Radical Criminology

issue two ★ fall 2013

ISSN: 1929-7904
ISBN: 978-0615877570

a publication of the
Critical Criminology Working Group
at Kwantlen Polytechnic University
(12666 - 72 Avenue, Surrey, BC V3W 2M8)
www.radicalcriminology.org

punctum books ✳ **brooklyn, ny**
http://www.punctumbooks.com

★ Radical Criminology ★ Issue 2 ★
September 2013 ★ ISSN 1929-7904

General Editor: Jeff Shantz

Production Editor: PJ Lilley

Advisory Board: Olga Aksyutina, Center for Civilizational and Regional Studies / Institute for African Studies of Russian Academy of Sciences, Moscow; **Davina Bhandar** (Trent U.); **Jeff Ferrell** (Texas Christian U.); **Hollis Johnson**, (Kwantlen Polytechnic U.); **Michael J. Lynch** (U. of South Florida); **Mike CK Ma**, (Kwantlen Polytechnic U.); **Lisa Monchalin**, (Kwantlen Polytechnic U.); **Heidi Rimke**, (U.Winnipeg); **Jeffrey Ian Ross**, (U.Baltimore)

cover art: Erin Marie Konsmo

layout & design: PJ Lilley

Unless otherwise stated, contributions express the opinions of their writers and are not (necessarily) those of the Editors or Advisory Board. Please visit our website for more information.

★ Contact Us ★

email: editors@radicalcriminology.org

website: http://journal.radicalcriminology.org

Mailing address: Kwantlen Polytechnic University, ATTN: Jeff Shantz, Dept. of Criminology 12666 72 Avenue | Surrey, BC, Canada V3W 2M8

★

In this period of state-sponsored austerity and suppression of resistance there is a great need for criminologists to speak out and act against state violence, state-corporate crime, and the growth of surveillance regimes and the prison-industrial complex. Criminologists also have a role to play in advancing alternatives to current regimes of regulation and punishment. In light of current social struggles against neoliberal capitalism, and as an effort to contribute positively to those struggles, the Critical Criminology Working Group at Kwantlen Polytechnic University in Vancouver has initiated this open access journal, *Radical Criminology*. We now welcome contributions. (See back page or our website for more details.)

Future issues might include:

Prison Abolition • Anti-colonialism • Resistance to Borders & Securitization • Surveillance and the Digital Panopticon • Anti-capitalism & Corporate Crime • the Military-Industrial Complex

This is not simply a project of critique, but is geared toward a praxis of struggle, insurgence and practical resistance.

★

Readers are welcome, and contributors are requested to keep in touch by signing up at
http://journal.radicalcriminology.org

Our website uses the Open Journal System,
developed by the Public Knowledge Project at
Simon Fraser University:

journal.radicalcriminology.org

Here, you may create your own profile to contribute to this
project, or simply subscribe your email address to our low traffic
mailing list, to receive notifications of important new content
added to the journal. Use of your address is limited to matters
relating to the journal, and we will not be sharing our
subscribers list with other organizations.

✶

As an online, open access publication,
all our content is freely available to all researchers
worldwide ensuring maximum dissemination.

Printed paper copies with full color cover
are available at cost through

punctum books ✶ brooklyn, ny
http://www.punctumbooks.com

"SPONTANEOUS ACTS OF SCHOLARLY COMBUSTION"

punctum books is an "open-access and print-on-
demand independent publisher dedicated to radically
creative modes of intellectual inquiry and writing
across a whimsical para-humanities assemblage."

Inside

editorial /

features /

arts /

insurgencies /

book reviews /

Editorial:
In Defense of Radicalism

In the present period few terms or ideas have been as slandered, distorted, diminished, or degraded as radical or radicalism. This is perhaps not too surprising given that this is a period of expanding struggles against state and capital, oppression and exploitation, in numerous global contexts. In such contexts, the issue of radicalism, of effective means to overcome power (or stifle resistance) become pressing. The stakes are high, possibilities for real alternatives being posed and opposed. In such contexts activists and academics must not only adequately understand radicalism, but defend (and advance) radical approaches to social change and social justice.

The first known use of the term radical is in the 14th century, 1350–1400; Middle English coming from Late Latin *rādīcālis*, having roots. It is also defined as being very different from the usual or traditional. The term radical simply means of or going to the roots or origin. Thoroughgoing. Straightforwardly, it means getting to the root of a problem.

Radicalism is a perspective, an orientation in the world. It is not, as is often mistakenly claimed, a strategy. To be radical is to dig beneath the surface of taken for granted assumptions, too easy explanations, unsatisfactory answers, and panaceas that pose as solutions to problems. Radicalism challenges and opposes status quo definitions—it refuses the self-serving justifications offered up by authority and power.

Rather than a set of ideas or actions, this is a crucial approach to life. As the existential Marxist analyst Erich Fromm has suggested in an earlier context of struggle:

> To begin with this approach can be characterized by the motto: *de omnibus dubitandum*; everything must be doubted, particularly the ideological concepts which are virtually shared by everybody and

have consequently assumed the role of indubitable common-sensi-
cal axioms...Radical doubt is a process; a process of liberation
from idolatrous thinking; a widening of awareness, of imaginative,
creative vision of our possibilities and options. The radical approach does not occur in a vacuum. It does not start from nothing,
but it starts from the roots. (1971, vii)

As is true for much of views and practices in class divided capitalist society, there are two distinct perspectives on radicalism,
two meanings of radicalism. From the first perspective of radicalism as a getting to the roots—going to the source of problems
—the nature of capital must be understood, addressed, confronted—overcome. Ending capital's violence can only be achieved
by ending the processes essential to its existence: exploitation,
expropriation, dispossession, profit, extraction, possession of the
commons, of nature. And how can this be accomplished? Capital
and states know—they understand. Thus, the identification of
those acts outlined above—identified, precisely, as radical.

Radicalism, from below, is sociological (and should be criminological, though criminology has sometimes lagged). It ex-
presses that orientation to the world espoused by C Wright Mills
as the sociological imagination (1959). Radicalism in its first
sense connects history, economy, politics, geography, culture,
seeking to move beyond the easy answers rigidified unreflexively as "common sense" (which is often neither common nor sensible). It digs beneath convention and the status quo. For Fromm:

> To "doubt" in this sense does not imply a psychological state of in-
> ability to arrive at decisions or convictions, as is the case in obses-
> sional doubt, but the readiness and capacity for critical questioning
> of all assumptions and institutions which have become idols under
> the name of common sense, logic, and what is supposed to be "nat-
> ural." (1971, viii)

More than that, radicalism does not seek nor take comfort in the
constructed moralism peddled by power—by state and capital.
A radical orientation does not accept the false moralism that de-
fines the acceptability of actions by their acceptability to powerholders or elites (law and order, rights of states, property
rights, and so on). As Fromm has stated it:

> This radical questioning is possible only if one does not take the
> concepts of one's own society or even of an entire historical period
> —like Western culture since the Renaissance—for granted, and fur-
> thermore if one enlarges the scope of one's awareness and pene-

trates into the unconscious aspects of one's thinking. Radical doubt is an act of uncovering and discovering; it is the dawning of the awareness that the Emperor is naked, and that his splendid garments are nothing but the product of one's phantasy. (1971, viii)

Breaking the law (of states, property) can be straightforwardly just and reasonable. As upholding the law can be (is, by definition) an act of acceptance of systems of injustice and violence. The hungry do not need to justify their efforts to feed themselves. The dispossessed do not need to explain their attempts to house themselves. The brutalized do not need to seek permission to stop brutality. If their efforts are radical—as they know it to mean—real solutions to real problems—then, so be it.

On other hand is the hegemonic definition asserted by capital (and its state servants). In this view, distorted through power's prism, radicalism is a word for extremism (chaos, disorder, violence, irrationality). Working class resistance, social movements, indigenous struggles, peasant uprisings, direct actions, and insurrections in urban centers—all opposition that challenges (or even calls into question) property relations, systems of command and control, exploitation of labor, theft of common resources by private interests—are defined by state and capital as radicalism, by which they mean extremism, or increasingly, terrorism.

All means of state authority control are thrown at containing or stamping out this radicalism—it is a large part of why modern police, criminal justice systems, and prisons, as well as the modern military, were created, developed, and expanded. In addition, and less remarked upon, are the "soft" practices of state and capital such as the psy industries which have long included rebelliousness as among the maladies requiring diagnosis and treatment.[1] As radical pedagogical theorist Ivan Illich suggests: "True testimony of profound nonconformity arouses the fiercest violence against it" (1971, 16). Such is the case in the current context of social struggles, and the repression deployed by state and capital to stamp out meaningful resistance (and frighten off soft support).

Yet the views and practices targeted in this construction of radicalism are really simply those that challenge and contest states and capital and offer alternative social relations. Even

---

[1] For more analysis on this, see Heidi Rimke's on-going work (2011, 2003)

where these movements pose little or no harm to anyone, even where they are explicitly non-violent (as in workplace occupations, strikes, indigenous land reclamations), power poses these activities as radical and extreme (and by association violent). This is really because such activities raise the specter of the first understanding of radicalism—that which comes from below—that which speaks to the perspectives of the oppressed and exploited. That definition is, in fact, true to the roots of the word and consistent with its meaning.

The charge of radicalism by powerholders, the question of radicalism itself, always becomes more prominent in periods of growing struggle. It is in those periods in which state capital has something to be concerned about. No longer are attempts to get to the roots consigned to the margins of social discourse, but that is what power seeks—to stuff it back into a place of control and regulation. In periods of low struggle the issue of radicalism is less often posed. That says something about the nature of the debates over radicalism.

Radicalism of the first meaning is not a kneejerk reaction to social conditions. For Illich, one must learn to distinguish "between destructive fury and the demand for radically new forms" (1971, 122). Where it takes apart, it takes apart in order to build. There is a need to "distinguish between the alienated mob and profound protest" (1971, 122–123). In Fromm's perspective:

> Radical doubt means to question; it does not necessarily mean to negate. It is easy to negate by simply positing the opposite of what exists; radical doubt is dialectical inasmuch as it comprehends the unfolding of oppositions and aims at a new synthesis which negates *and* affirms. (1971, viii)

As the anarchist Mikhail Bakunin has suggested, the passion to destroy is also a creative passion.

Issues of extremism, introduced by powerholders to serve their power, are a diversion, a red herring so to speak. Supposedly extreme or outrageous acts are not necessarily radical, as is suggested in mass media that often treat them as synonymous. Extreme acts (and more needs to be said about this misleading term) that fail to get to the roots of state capital relations, such as misguided acts of violence against civilians, are not radical. They do not get to the root of capitalist exploitation (even if frustration over exploitation gives rise to them). Acts that only serve to reinforce relations of repression or legitimize state initiatives are not radical.

At the same time, some extreme acts are radical. These acts should be judged on their real impact on state capitalist power, on institutions of exploitation and oppression.

Within the state capitalist context extremism is rendered devoid of meaning. In a system founded on, and subsisting on mass murder, genocide, and ecocide as the everyday reality of its existence, notions of extremism become irrelevant, nonsensical. Particularly when used trivially, flippantly, to describe minor acts of opposition or resistance, even desperation. In this context, too, the issue of violence (in a society founded on, underpinned by everyday acts of extreme violence) or non-violence is something of a phony construction (one favorable to power which legitimizes its own violence or poses violent acts like exploitation as non-violent), a rigged game.

Power never admits its own extremism, its own violence, its own chaos, destruction, disorder. The disorder of inequality, the chaos of dispossession, the destruction of traditional or indigenous communities and relationships—the extermination of survival, of the planet itself. These are real extremist behaviors. They are, in fact endemic to the exercise of power within state capitalist societies.

The destruction of entire ecosystems for the profit of a few is a ferociously "rational" act (against the irrationality of radical approaches to stop such devastation). The extinguishing of entire communities—the genocide of peoples—to secure land and resources is an unspeakably extreme action, in ecological and human terms. Yet power never identifies this as at all radical—it is always simply a fact of life, a cost of doing business, a side effect of necessary progress, an unfortunate outcome of history (with no one responsible).

And these are not even the extremes, not even rare outliers of capitalism—these are the foundational acts of capital's being—they are the nature of capital. Colonial conquest, for example, is not an unfortunate side effect or excess of capitalism—it is its very possibility, its essence.

Activists who fail to get to the root of social or ecological problems—who fail to understand what radicalism from below means for resistance—can be, and generally are, too readily enlisted by state capital in the hegemonic chorus that assails and condemns, that slanders and besmirches radicalism. We see this in the context of alternative globalization movements in which some activists, claiming non-violent civil disobedience (NVCD) ahistorically, without context, as if it is some sort of fetish object, who then join the police, politicians, corporations, and mass media in condemning direct action, blockades, street occupations, barricades, or, of course, property damage, as being too radical—as acts of violence. The voices of anti-radical activists becomes a part of the delegitimation of resistance itself, a key aspect in the maintenance of power and inequality.

Such public disavowals of resistance serve to justify, excuse, and maintain the very real violence that *is* capital. Perspectives, including those of activists, that condemn resistance, including, for example, armed resistance, are simply enabling apologizing for, justifying the continued and expanded (it always expands in the absence of real opposition) violence of state capital.

Survival is not a crime. Survival is *never* radical. Exploitation is *always* a crime (or should be). Exploitation is *only ever* the norm of capitalist social relations.

Powerholders will always seek to discredit or delegitimize resistance to their privilege and deployment of loaded (misconstructed and misconstrued by powerholders) terms like radicalism will be a tactic in this. One can follow the reconstruction of the term "terror" to see an example of such processes. The term 'terror' was initially used to designate state violence deployed against anyone deemed to be a threat to instituted authority, to the state. (Badiou 2011, 17) Only later—as an outcome of hegemonic struggle—did terror come (for state powerholders) to designate actions of civilians—even actions *against* the state.

And it often works. Certainly, it has played a part in the dampening or softening of potentialities for alternative globalization movements, as has been the case in previous periods of struggle. In this such anti-radical activists inevitably bolster state capitalist power and authority and reinforce injustice.

Yet we need to be optimistic as well. The charge of radicalism from above (assertive on the surface) is also a cry for help on behalf of power. It is a plea by power to the non-committal sectors, the soft middle, to tilt away from the resisting sectors and side with power (states and capital) in re-asserting the status quo (or extending relations and practices they find beneficial, a new status quo of privilege)—the conditions of conquest and exploitation.

Radicalism (or extremism, or terrorism) is the charge used by power to quell unrest by drawing support toward the ruling interests. In that sense it suggests a certain desperation on behalf of the powerful—one that should be seized upon, not played into or alleviated.

In periods of rising mass struggles, the issue of radicalism is inevitably posed. It is in these times that a radical orientation breaks through the confines of hegemonic legitimation—posing new questions, better answers, and real alternatives. To oppose radicalism is to oppose thought itself. To oppose radicalism is to accept the terms set out by power, to limit oneself to that which power will allow.

Anti-radicalism is inherently elitist and anti-democratic. It assumes that everyone, regardless of status, has access to channels of political and economic decision-making, and can participate in meaningful ways to address personal or collective needs. It overlooks the exclusion of vast segments of the population from decisions that most impact their lives and the unequal access to social resources that necessitate, that impel, radical changes.

Activists, as well as sociologists and criminologists, must defend radicalism from below as the necessary orientation to struggle against injustice, exploitation, and oppression and for alternative social relations. Actions should be assessed not according to a legal moral framework provided by and reinforced by state capital (for their own benefit). Assessment should be made on real impacts in ending (or hastening the end of) injustice, exploitation, and oppression, on the weakening of state capital. As Martin Luther King suggested, a riot is simply the language of the unheard.

Self-righteous moralizing and reference to legal authority, parroting the voices of state capital, is an abdication of social responsibility for activists. For sociologists and criminologists it is an abandonment of the sociological imagination which in its emphasis on getting to the roots of issues has always been radical (in the non-hegemonic sense). Critical thinkers and actors of all stripes must defend this radicalism. They must become radicals themselves.

Debates should focus on the effectiveness of perspectives and practices in getting to the roots of social problems, of uprooting power. They should not center on fidelity to the law or bourgeois morality. They should not be constrained by the lack of imagination of participants or by the sense that the best of all worlds is the world that power has proposed.

Again, radicalism is not a tactic, an act, an event. It is not a matter of extremes, in a world that takes horrifying extremes for granted. It is an orientation to the world. The features of radicalism are determined by, and in, specific contexts. This is the case now in the context of mass mobilizations, even popular uprisings against statist austerity offensives in the service of neoliberal capitalism. Radicalism always threatens to overflow attempts to contain it. It is because it advances understanding—poses social injustice in stark relief—that it is by nature re/productive. It is, in current terms, viral.

Jeff Shantz, Salt Spring Island, Summer 2013

REFERENCES

Badiou, Alain. 2011. *Polemics*. London: Verso

Fromm, Erich. 1971. "Introduction." *Celebration of Awareness: A Call for Institutional Revolution*. New York: Doubleday Anchor

Illich, Ivan. 1971. Celebration of Awareness: A Call for Institutional Revolution. New York: Doubleday Anchor

Mills, C. Wright. 1959. *The Sociological Imagination*. London: Oxford University Press.

Rimke, Heidi. 2011. "The Pathological Approach to Crime: Individually Based Theories." In *Criminology: Critical Canadian Perspectives*, ed. Kirsten Kramar. Toronto: Pearson Education Canada, 78-92

———. 2003 "Constituting Transgressive Interiorities: C19th Psychiatric Readings of Morally Mad Bodies." In *Violence and the Body: Race, Gender and the State*, ed. A. Arturo. Indiana: Indiana University Press, 403-28

[features]

The Earth Liberation Front: A Social Movement Analysis

MICHAEL LOADENTHAL[1]

ABSTRACT

The Earth Liberation Front is a radical environmental movement that developed from the ideological factionalization of the British Earth First! movement of the 1990s. Its ideological underpinnings are based in deep ecology, anti-authoritarian anarchism highlighting a critique of capitalism, a commitment to non-violence, a collective defense of the Earth, and a warranted feeling of persecution by State forces. In its current form, the Earth Liberation Front is a transnational, decentralized network of clandestine, autonomous, cells that utilize illegal methods of protest by sabotaging and vandalizing property. The small unit cells are self-contained entities that can operate without the support of external entities such as financiers or weapons procurers. Tactical and operational knowledge is developed and shared through commercially available books written by the broader environmental movement throughout the last four decades, as well as inter-movement publications produced by the cells and distributed through numerous sympathetic websites. Membership can be understood as occurring on two levels, the covert cell level and the public support level, both of which operate

---

[1] Michael Loadenthal is a doctoral candidate and adjunct professor who finds himself stranded between Cincinnati and Washington, DC, multi-tasking as a father, conspirator and writer. Over the past 15 years he has organized amongst a variety of global direct action movements and at present is conducting top secret research for The Revolution. He can be reached at michael.loadenthal@gmail.com and mloadenthal.wordpress.com.

in tandem to produce and publicize acts of property destruction.   At the cell level, individuals conduct pre-operational reconnaissance and surveillance, develop and construct weapons systems, carry out orchestrated attacks, and announce their actions to support groups and media while maintaining internal security and anonymity.   At the aboveground level, support entities help to publicize attacks carried out by cells, respond to media inquiries and other public engagements, identify and coordinate aid to imprisoned cell members, and develop and distribute sympathetic propaganda produced by, and in support of affiliated individuals.   This case study uses the history of the Earth Liberation Front's United States attacks as its unit of analysis, and seeks to outline the ideology, structure, context and membership factors that constitute the movement.

INTRODUCTION

October 14 is Columbus Day, a national holiday in the United States when citizens are reminded of their colonial roots. On this day in 1996, the Earth Liberation Front (ELF) leapt into action in the US state of Oregon. In one night, individuals carried out three simultaneous attacks targeting a Chevron station, a public relations office and a McDonald's restaurant. All three targets had their locks glued and their property painted with political messages including a three letter calling card, E.L.F. (Molland 2006, 55). For the US, this was the first salvo from the ELF, a clandestine, decentralized network of autonomous cells using sabotage and vandalism to cause financial hardship to targets thought to be abusing the Earth. From this small action, less than ten years later, the US would declare the ELF "the most active criminal extremist element in the United States" (Lewis 2004) and the "number one domestic terrorist threat"[2] (Schuster 2005). While such rhetoric was mobilized with great strength in the decade following the millennium, the ELF remains active, transitory and for the most part, resistant to discovery and arrest.

---

[2] A lengthy analysis of the post-9/11 rhetoric of terrorism deployed against environmental and animal liberation activists is the subject of an article recent published by this author (Loadenthal 2013) entitled "Deconstructing 'Eco-Terrorism': Rhetoric, Framing and Statecraft as Seen Through the Insight Approach," appearing in the journal *Critical Studies on Terrorism*, Vol. 6, Issue 1.

The ELF is often discussed in tandem alongside other environmental and animal liberation/rights-focused movements as the main actors engaging in "eco-terrorism," defined as:

> The use or threatened use of violence of a criminal nature against innocent victims or property by an environmentally orientated subnational group for environmental-political reasons, aimed at an audience beyond the target, and often of a symbolic nature. (Eagan 1996, 2)

Broadly, this definition fails to define the ELF as it does not employ violence against "innocent victims." In the framing of "innocent victims" versus "property" noted above, one presumes that *victims* refers to *humans*, and as such, the ELF defies this definitional description as it has sought to damage property, not humans, and has managed to avoid injuring individuals accidentally. (Borum and Tilby 2005, 212; Leader and Probst 2003, 44; Taylor 1998, 3, 8)   As one scholar familiar with the "eco-terrorist" history writes, "While the ELF has caused millions of dollars worth of property damage, it has not yet intentionally (or even unintentionally) brought harm to anyone". (Ackerman 2003, 162)   Such a casualty-free history should be noted as with nearly 300 attacks[3] claimed globally from 1996-2009 (Loadenthal 2010, 81), not a single human has been killed or injured (Loadenthal 2010, 98). In its 290 attacks claimed at the ELF, and its 69 attacks (Loadenthal 2010, 81) claimed jointly with the Animal Liberation Front (ALF), the target has always been property.

What follows is a case study analysis of the ELF movement as it operated (1996-2009) in North America. The majority of evidence presented is taken from centrist, state-affiliated, security-themed sources[4] whose purpose is to identify, locate and

---

[3] All quantitate data of this variety are taken from a previously completed study (Loadenthal 2010) of the larger field of "eco-terrorism" completed in 2010 as part of the author's MLitt dissertation completed while studying at the Centre For the Study of Terrorism and Political Violence at the University of St Andrews. This research included an incident-based, quantitate analysis of 27,136 incidents of "eco-terrorism" occurring in over 40 countries from 1972-2010. Each incident was passed through a decision tree, and if included in the data set, coded for 22 variables and analyzed with the Statistical Package for the Social Sciences (SPSS) software program.

[4] See for example (109th Congress 2005; Ackerman 2003; Anti-Defamation League 2005; Borum and Tilby 2005; Chalk 2001; FBI Counterterrorism and

capture activists. While many of these sources make specious claims regarding activists' behaviors, they remain the most often quoted, 'authoritative' sources on the subject. For this reason the majority of the facts established herein will be adopted from such security-industry forces as to produce a descriptive social movement account that is both informed by a radical analysis, and triangulated with facts established by the State and its largess of resources and affiliated institutions.

Whereas the ELF is a global movement, with cells active in more than twenty countries, for the purpose of this analysis, cases will be limited to their North American attacks, the vast majority of which occurred in the continental US. Other affiliated radical networks and movements, such as the ALF and Earth First! (EF!) will be discussed as they relate to the history and developmental context of the ELF. This study is an attempt to paint a holistic picture of the ELF as a social movement, examining its ideology, structure, context, and multi-tiered membership that collectively constitute its ranks.

This study seeks neither to prove nor dispel a testable hypothesis, but rather to develop a detailed picture of the ELF's praxis as developed via its US activity. The study utilizes the US ELF movement as its unit of analysis (Yin 2008, 22–23), and seeks to explore the movement's philosophical underpinnings, networks, the context leading to its development, and the characteristics of its membership. The evidence presented herein is a synthesis of open source documentation, archival records and academic journals as well as numerous inter-movement publications authored by pro-ELF organizations. Whenever possible triangulation of data has been achieved and demonstrated through the multi-sourcing of findings via scholarly studies, government reports and inter-movement publications. (Yin 2008, 91–92)

A BRIEF HISTORY

Beginning in the 1960s, a political movement emerged advancing a radically new critique of environmental and animal use

---

Cyber Divisions 2004; Helios Global, Inc. 2008; Immergut et al. 2007; Jackson and Frelinger 2008; Jarboe 2002; Taylor 2003; Trujillo 2005)

practices. These new ideological tendencies were characterized by not only a shift in philosophical outlook, but also in language and collective practice. This time period is often associated with the founding of the *deep ecology* framework, authored by Norwegian philosopher Arne Næss in 1972 (Eagan 1996, 3), replacing the environmental protectionism of past, as well as ideas of *animal liberation,* inspired by a 1975 book of the same title by Peter Singer. Just as Singer's notion of *liberation* replaced previously popular notions of animal *welfare* or *rights*, the groups which formed during this time replaced previously dominant strategies of collective popular protest with that of self-guided, autonomous units. These new revolutionary frameworks were quickly adopted by emergent groups, which began to utilize sabotage, vandalism and arson.

1963 saw the formation of the Hunt Saboteurs Association, dedicated to physically disrupting hunting expeditions, often taking the form of sabotage and provocation. After working with a group of hunt saboteurs in the early 1970s, several activists decided to shift their tactical focus. In 1972, the Band of Mercy (BOM) formed in England as the outgrowth of desire for a new praxis that prioritized taking animals out of harm's way, as well as financially sabotaging companies and institutions contributing to animal exploitation. Within three years of its founding, the BOM morphed into what has historically been the most active, clandestine, direct action group, the ALF. Since its founding in England in 1976, the ALF has carried out thousands of attacks globally. Several years after the formation of the ALF, the movement witnessed a factionalization into smaller, more violence-prone splinter cells and experienced deterritorialization to over forty countries. By 1994, the ALF inspired the formation of an organizationally and tactically similar movement targeting institutions of *ecological* exploitation through methods of sabotage and vandalism—the ELF. Throughout thirty-eight years under examination, the BOM, ALF and ELF have further deterritorialized and led to the formation of at least three hundred similarly-styled groups. This global movement of movements which opposes violence (toward animals and the environment) has garnered the label 'eco-terrorism' from governments, media, and elements of the academic community.

POLITICAL-PHILOSOPHICAL IDEOLOGY

In establishing the ELF's ideology, we examine movement literature produced through aboveground support networks, such as the North American ELF Press Office[5] (NAELFPO). In a 2001 pamphlet, the NAELFPO states that "if an individual believes in the ideology and follows a certain set of guidelines she or he can perform actions and become a part of the ELF" (North American Earth Liberation Front Press Office 2001, 3). In a similar fashion to the ALF, these "guidelines" are established by unknown persons and distributed through movement literature thus creating a discursive reality for subsequent action. While there is no central authority that then judges actions to be in agreement with or in violation of the guideline, movement debate and discussion serves as a vetting process. According to the NAELFPO pamphlet, "Frequently Asked Question About the Earth Liberation Front," (2001) the group's guidelines are:

> 1) To cause as much economic damage as possible to a given entity that is profiting off the destruction of the natural environment and life for selfish greed and profit,

> 2) To educate the public on the atrocities committed against the environment and life,

> 3) To take all necessary precautions against harming life.

Such broad-based guidelines serve a functional purpose allowing for great tactical and strategic diversity while avoiding the factionalizing function (Joosse 2007) of public debate regarding the legitimacy of every action taken under the ELF moniker. Thus is an action is carried out, it is up to the activists to decide to either adopt the ELF name or not.

The "ideology" of the ELF contains thematic trends collectively constituting a shared ethos. Firstly, "deep ecology", often termed biocentrism, that teaches all living entities, human and non-human, have equal worth and value and an *inherent*

---

[5] The NAELFPO has at times gone silent for larger periods. After being established in 1999, it maintained an active web presence for years before going offline, and the reestablishing itself in 2008. At present, in 2013, the site is once again offline.

right to exist and prosper. It is through this lens that the ELF understands its position *vis-à-vis* those understood to be destroying the Earth. Some of this influence comes from the ELF's historical development alongside anarchism, and specifically its anti-civilization tendencies often termed Green anarchism, anarcho-primitivism or simply, Primitivism. (Taylor 2003, 181) At this juncture, the *greening* of anarchism extends its typically anthropocentric analysis towards deep ecology. (Ackerman 2003, 147; The Green Anarchy Collective 2009)[6] Green anarchism advocates the creation of a collectivized, pre-industrial, "wild" civilization of loosely affiliated, village-sized communities, devoid of modern industry and technology. (Eagan 1996, 3–4; Helios Global, Inc. 2008, 4–5; Leader and Probst 2003, 40) The ELF ideology borrows heavily from anarchism, and as such, a great number of anarchists fill the ranks of the movement. (Borum and Tilby 2005, 208; Leader and Probst 2003, 40; Taylor 2003, 181) The philosophical teachings of anarchism and the ELF concur that all forms of oppression are inherently incompatible with human society and must be replaced with non-hierarchical, non-coercive methods of organization and collective responsibility. (Ackerman 2003, 147; Leader and Probst 2003, 40) This philosophical understanding opposing hierarchal structures, is reflected in the ELF's organizational methods. (Chalk 2001; Eagan 1996, 2; Trujillo 2005, 146) Closely linked, the ELF shares a great deal with the broad leftist movements often termed, "anti-corporate/globalization," or "anti-capitalist" (Ackerman 2003, 153; Leader and Probst 2003, 40; Trujillo 2005, 159). Radical environmentalists share ideology with these movements arguing that modern capitalism "represents the single most important threat to the...environment," (Helios Global, Inc. 2008, 5) and that Western-led individualism is *predicated* on the exploitation of the natural resources of the Earth. (Ackerman 2003, 146; Helios Global, Inc. 2008, 4)

Secondly, the ELF claims to act as the "voice of the voiceless," the "defender of the defenseless," arguing that the planet is the victim of attacks perpetuated by mankind, for which it

---

[6] The politics and philosophy of anarcho-primitivism have been developed and popularized by writers such as John Zerzan, Kevin Tucker, Bob Black, John Moore, Derrick Jenson, and infamously by Theodore Kaczynski, better known as the "Unabomber."

cannot respond in voice nor action (Ackerman 2003, 146–147; Helios Global, Inc. 2008, 4). The inability of the Earth to speak for itself empowers the ELF to speak and act in its defense (North American Earth Liberation Front Press Office 2001, 4) despite such a anthropocentric protectionism being challenged[7] by critical activists. Thirdly, the ELF advocates non-violence as it relates to all forms of life, simultaneously denying that non-living entities such as the property of eco-offenders, corporations, governments, etc. also have an inherent protection from violence (Eagan 1996, 9; Leader and Probst 2003, 41; North American Earth Liberation Front Press Office 2001, 27–28). This understanding and consistent injury-free practice allows the ELF to frame its acts of property destruction as non-violent sabotage, as such actions fail to target living creatures. (jones 2006, 324)

Lastly, ELF ideology is tinged with accusations of unjustified attack by law enforcement. (Ackerman 2003, 146; Eagan 1996, 13) This theme is commonly cited in communiqués from ELF cells as many believe they are being maliciously persecuted by governments. Such accusatory posturing by the ELF in their criticism of the State is certainly deserved. Since the US began its Domestic War on Terrorism following the attacks of September 11, 2001, environmental and animal liberation activists have become the target of increased State repression (Loadenthal 2013; Lovitz 2010; Potter 2011; Slater 2011) in what activists have termed the Green Scare. Within this pursue to produce arrests, the State has utilized a host of repressive methods not typically deployed amongst non-violence social movements. Included in its arsenal targeting direct action animal and earth liberationists is the use of state[8] and federal-level legislation (e.g. Animal Enterprise Terrorism Act, Ag-Gag legislation), the placement of police informants and provocateurs (such as the case of Eric McDavid and Marie Mason), home raids and other militarized forms of overt policing, increased electronic surveillance, use of Grand Juries to coerce informa-

---

[7] See for example (Loadenthal 2012) wherein this author challenges the human-centric notion of protectionism offered by animal/earth liberation activists who claim to be speaking for the oppressed non-human animals and 'natural' world.

[8] Such as Pennsylvania's "Ecoterrorism - 18 Pa. Cons. Stat. § 3311"

tion, and the use of anti-terrorist prison facilities to house inmates (such as the case of Daniel McGowan, Andrew Stepanian, Stanislas Meyerhoff and Walter Bond)[9]. The largess of the State's targeted repression of such activists has been well established in activist scholarship and as such is not the focus of this investigation.

TACTICAL IDEOLOGY

The ELF extends its framework establishing tactical methodology melding philosophy with practice, creating a radical, anti-State, anti-capitalist, environmental praxis. This praxis advocates "direct action," (Helios Global, Inc. 2008, 12) to "remove the profit motive from killing the Earth" (North American Earth Liberation Front Press Office 2001, 28). Direct action, a key component of the anarchist tradition, is seen as the only way to achieve the ELF aims as traditional methods of politicking and lobbying have failed to achieve rapid success (Trujillo 2005, 146). For the ELF, direct action constitutes the use of illegal means of political protest such as sabotage, arson and other manners of property destruction to economically damage entities established as its enemies. In this sense, the ELF's goal is the financially insolvency of its targets using economic sabotage. To this end, the ELF advocates the use of methods (termed 'weapon technologies' in the Terrorism/Security Studies literature) that cause financial harm while avoiding harming humans, animals and the environment. The weapons socio-political groups choose provide insight into their politics, as "the specific weapons technologies groups choose...[and]...define the scale and scope of their violence" (Jackson and Frelinger 2008, 583). For the ELF there is a focuses on improvised incendiaries (Jackson and Frelinger 2008, 597–598) self-manufactured from modified, off-the-shelf items (Helios Global, Inc. 2008, 26), guided by instruction from movement publications distributed mainly through the internet. (109th Congress 2005,

---

[9] A detailed exploration of the methods employed in the Green Scare is the subject of a book chapter written by the author to be published in late 2013 entitled "The 'Green Scare' & 'Eco-Terrorism': The Development of US Counter-Terrorism Strategy Targeting Direct Action Activists." Published in *The Law Against Animals: A Challenge to the Animal Enterprise Terrorism Act.* Eds. Jason Del Gandio, Et al. Forthcoming. Lantern Press, 2013.

44; Joosse 2007, 354) The decision to use incendiaries, as opposed to firearms or projectiles, reflects ELF's desire to damage property while avoiding causalities. (Jackson and Frelinger 2008, 598)

The ELF's targeting ideology reflects its desire to cause financial hardship whilst avoiding causalities and generally, chooses target such as "facilities and companies involved in logging, genetic engineering, home building, automobile sales, energy production and distribution" (Leader and Probst 2003, 43). Targets chosen by cells are understood to be *directly* damaging the environment. Also contributing to the ELF's targeting decisions is the amount of security their targets employ. The ELF tends to attack targets that are not hardened against attack such as those affiliated with commercial business, University research and residential housing as opposed to more heavily protected targets such as military sites, government facilities or heavy industrial or manufacturing facilities.   Therefore homes under construction are targeted, not realtors. (North American Earth Liberation Front Press Office 2009b)[10] Privately owned vehicles are targeted, not car manufacturers. (North American Earth Liberation Front Press Office 2009c)[11] Genetically engineered organisms (GMO) are pulled from the ground, and research centers destroyed with fire. (North American Earth Liberation Front Press Office 2009a)[12] In these examples, the targeting reflects the desire to *directly* target the perceived ills, not to remedy them through attacking intermediary or secondary target.   When examined through a global incident-based, quantitative analysis, one discovers that the ELF's main target types are construction and industrial equipment

---

[10] September 19, 2003, an ELF cell burned down four luxury homes and damaged three others in San Diego, California's Carmel Valley neighborhood. A banner was left at the scene of the arson that read, "Development destruction. Stop raping nature. The ELFs are angry."

[11] May 17, 2006 an ELF cell damaged six SUVs in Fair Oaks, California by slashing the vehicles' tires and using spray paint to write "ELF" on the vehicles.

[12] December 31, 1999 an ELF cell severely damaged a research center at Michigan State University's Lansing campus because the University was conducting genetic engineering research in conjunction with GE-advocate Monsanto and the United States Agency for International Development. The fire causes $900,000 in damages.

(14%), model homes and homes under construction (13%), business properties (12%) and automobiles most often sport utility vehicles (10)%. (Loadenthal 2010) Other target types include (in descending order of frequency) phone booths, private business vehicles, farms, ranches and breeders, GMU crops and government property including vehicles.

STRUCTURE—ORGANIZATIONAL NETWORK

The ELF functions as a networked movement, not as an organization. It is a decentralized collection of autonomously operating, small unit, clandestine cells without organizational hierarchy or command and control structure.(Helios Global, Inc. 2008, 1, 8, 11) Thus, "ELF" is a name given to the sum total of attacks carried out by disconnected cells and 'lone wolf' attackers. It is an adoptable moniker for whomever wishes to use it. Whereas ELF cells may share a basic philosophical-political critique, generally cells have no communication or cooperation amongst themselves. In some isolated cases, operation coordination, or at least communication has likely occurred between cells. For example, on May 21, 2001, two ELF cells carried out simultaneous arsons targeting the Jefferson Poplar Farms in Clatskaine, Oregon and the horticulture research laboratory of the University of Washington in Seattle, Washington. According to the Federal Bureau of Investigations (FBI), both ELF cell responsible for the arsons were part of a twenty person multi-cell unit of the ELF known as "the family." Eleven members of "the family" were arrested by the FBI during "Operation Backfire" in late 2005 and early 2006, and linked to seventeen attacks in Oregon, Wyoming, Washington, California, and Colorado. From open source information, it is impossible to determine how common such multi-cell entities are within the greater milieu of the ELF movement. Law enforcement have found cells extremely difficult to infiltrate (Helios Global, Inc. 2008, 11) reporting that most possess "sophisticated organization and operational security," (Ackerman 2003, 151) including knowledge of forensics, signals intelligence, computer security, cryptography and police surveillance. (109th Congress 2005, 44; FBI Counterterrorism and Cyber Divisions 2004, 2–4; Immergut et al. 2007, 5, 35, 102, 117, 123, 134; Leader and Probst 2003, 42; Trujillo 2005, 154–155, 163) Cells operate

with no known external support structure, existing self-suffi-
ciently, fulfilling their logistical, funding, intelligence and
weapons acquisition needs. Unlike traditional terrorist organizations and violent non-State actors, there is no need for ELF
cells to receive financial support from nation-states or smuggle
weapons through secretive networks. Attacks are self-funded
from the cell members as their cost is low. (Helios Global, Inc.
2008, 27) Additional tasks traditionally assigned to externals
are self-managed including pre-operational surveillance and reconnaissance, training and weapons acquisition. (Leader and
Probst 2003, 42)

Beyond the level of the cell, the ELF is understood as a
movement of "leaderless resistance," a style of decentralization
popularized by Louis Beam (1992), an American white suprem-
acist, who describes a leaderless resistance model as:

> ...A fundamental departure in theories of organization...[wherein]
> all individuals and groups operate independently of each other, and
> never report to a central headquarters or single leader for direction
> or instruction, as would those who belong to a typical pyramid or-
> ganization. (1992)

This leaderless resistance, with no centralized authority or command and control, is seen in the workings of the ELF. The
structure has great advantages for resisting infiltration by law
enforcement, and provides a simple means of cell replication.
The decentralized, autonomous, non-hierarchical network structure is also familiar to new members as it is the common organizational method within anarchist movements where many
ELF members are active. (Borum and Tilby 2005, 212; Chalk
2001) Due to the autonomy of the ELF cells, cells are not
aware of others, and existing cells cannot be joined. (Dishman
2005, 243) Because of their self-contained nature, new recruits
are encouraged to form their own cell. (Joosse 2007, 354) This
advice is given plainly in a NAELFPO (2001) pamphlet, wherein the author states:

> Individuals interested in becoming active in the ELF need to follow
> the above guidelines and create their own close knit anonymous cell
> made up of trustworthy and sincere people. Remember the ELF
> and each cell within it are anonymous not only to one another but
> also to the general public. So there is not a realistic chance of be-
> coming active in an already existing cell. Take initiative, form your

own cell and do what needs to be done to protect all life on the planet! (2001, 15)

The leaderless resistance structure provides the ELF with a number of benefits, besides operational security, most notably, the ability to avoid protracted ideological debate leading to stagnation and factionalization. Paul Joosse (2007) addresses this, writing:

> Leaderless resistance allows the ELF to avoid ideological cleavages by eliminating all ideology extraneous to the very specific cause of halting the degradation of nature...leaderless resistance creates an 'overlapping consensus' among those with vastly different ideological orientations, mobilizing a mass of adherents that would never been able to find unanimity of purpose in an organization characterized by a traditional, hierarchical, authority structure...[individuals can]...'believe what they will,' while mobilizing them to commit 'direct actions'. (2007, 352)

Leaderless resistance prevents factionalization, allowing divergent activists to appear unified despite ideological differences.

The independence of leaderless resistance contains the potentiality to damage the movement if cells act outside of stated policy. For example "a particularly militant splinter cell, a peripheral individual or...ad-hoc group" could carry out an attack attributed to the ELF but via means breaking from group tradition. (Ackerman 2003, 153) The ELF movement lacks the ability to prevent cells from committing lethal actions and claiming them in the movement's name, (Leader and Probst 2003, 42) other than arguing that its guidelines call for the taking of "necessary precautions against harming life". Such a tension is of growing relevance with a sudden surge in eco-affiliated, primitivist-themed attacks in countries such as Mexico, where networks such as Individuals Tending Toward the Wild have reportedly killed and injured targets attacked do to their role in biotechnology and the larger "Techno-Industrial System." This potential conflict for the ELF has yet to be tested, but provides a challenge for the network in preserving its records of avoiding human causalities. Despite this risk, the ELF's structure allows cells and individuals to act independently to set the agenda for the larger transnational movement (Joosse 2007, 356), thus the global ELF campaign is simply the collection of attacks carried out by autonomous entities.

STRUCTURE—ORGANIZATIONAL LEARNING

Due to the tendency for cells to act without support, the movement must uniquely develop tactical and operational skill sets. The ELF has addressed this, facilitating organizational learning through print text and internet. Many texts were the product of radical environmentalist movements led by EF! preceding the ELF's founding. (Leader and Probst 2003, 38)   From 1970-1980, numerous skills-based instructive texts, such as Ecodefense[13], emerged wherein readers were taught tactics utilized by the modern ELF including sabotage, arson, and internal security. (Eagan 1996, 8; FBI Counterterrorism and Cyber Divisions 2004, 2–4; Laqueur 2000, 203)[14]   Following an increase in internet access, the focus was shifted to online resources for cataloging technical and training material.   In his report for RAND, Horacio Trujillo (2005) writes:

> Operational learning has been facilitated by...the movement's use of published material, first in print and now via the Internet, to disseminate and store knowledge...Advances in information technology, particularly the Internet, have significantly increased the reach of these organizations' materials and have provided the ELF with the ability to disseminate training and logistics information. (2005, 153)

The ELF's main (now defunct) aboveground website, NAELFPO,[15] formerly acted as a clearinghouse for individuals looking

---

[13] A complete copy of the 3rd edition of Dave Foreman's book *Ecodefense: A Field Guide to Monkeywrenching*, is available online at http://www.omnipresence.mahost.org/inttxt.htm. In establishing the themes of this book, as discussed in the study, the text was accessed online, without page numbers, making item specific referencing impossible. The complete citation for the book can be found below:

Foreman, Dave. *Ecodefense: A Field Guide to Monkeywrenching*. 3rd edition. Chico: Abbzug Press, 1993.

[14] These skills-based texts of the time include *Ecodefense: A Field Guide to Monkeywrenching*, where readers are taught tactics utilized by the modern ELF including tree spiking, sabotage, arson, and internal security. Additional books also emerged at this time serving as guides to potential saboteurs including *The Black Cat Sabotage Handbook*, *EF! Direct Action Manual*, *Earthforce! An Earth Warrior's Guide to Strategy* and *Road Raging: Top Tips for Wrecking Roadbuilding*. A complete version of *Road Raging* is available at: http://www.eco-action.org/rr/

[15] Available at: http://www.elfpressoffice.org/

for links to sympathetic sites that host training materials. The NAELPO's site has been offline often for extended periods of time, but when active, receives a great deal of traffic partially due to heavy referencing in media accounts of attacks. Brigitte Nacos's (2006) discussion of terrorist groups' use of the internet makes this claim stating:

> Overblown media reports about arson attacks on new housing developments or gas-guzzling sports utility vehicles by the Earth Liberation Front familiarized the American public with the motives of this by and large negligible 'eco-terrorist' movement... the mainstream media helped interested persons to find the group's Internet site that serves as a recruitment tool and a how-to-commit-terrorism resource. (2006, 43)

As of the time of writing, the NAELFPO website has been down for some time, but despite this barrier, movement communiqués can still be viewed at affiliated English language sites such as Bite Back Magazine[16], the North American Animal Liberation Press Office[17], and a host of direct action/insurrectionary anarchist themed websites such as 325[18], War on Society[19], Act For Freedom Now! and Contra Info[20]. Through these websites and others in a host of foreign languages, individuals can access semi-centralized resources for publicizing attacks, reading communiqués from previous attacks, and learning operational skills such as security,[21] sabotage[22] and weapons production.[23]

---

[16] http://www.directaction.info/

[17] http://www.animalliberationpressoffice.org/index.htm

[18] http://325.nostate.net/

[19] http://waronsociety.noblogs.org/

[20] http://en.contrainfo.espiv.net/

[21] For an example see Activist Security v2.7, published June 2008 by www.ActivistSecurity.org. The NAELFPO website maintain an entire page on security (http://www.elfpressoffice.org/security.html) wherein they provide links to nearly 50 separate guides to issues of security including encryption, forensic, criminal investigation techniques and electronic surveillance.

[22] For an example, see Ozymandias Sabotage Handbook, available at http://www.reachoutpub.com/osh/ via the NAELFPO "resource" page.

[23] For example see Arson-Around with Auntie ALF: Your Guide to Putting Heat on Animal Abusers Everywhere or Setting Fires With Electrical Timers:

The weapons technology of the ELF, consists of of-f-the-shelf materials with dual usage[24] used to construct incendiaries. (Helios Global, Inc. 2008, 1, 26) Typical designs for improvised incendiary devices utilize widely available items such as alkaline batteries, kitchen/egg timers, basic electrical components, matches, road flares, model rocket igniters, filament light bulbs, alligator clips, granulated sugar, liquid hydrocarbon fuels (gasoline, diesel, oil, kerosene, etc.), paraffin, sawdust, incense sticks, sponges, tampons, plastic jugs, cigarette lighters, solder and insulated wire. Through the guidance provided by online guides[25] the ELF can develop organizational knowledge, distribute member instruction, and adapt new technologies as developments improves.[26] Beyond technical training and development, the internet also serves a variety of functions to establish a collectively crafted history of attacks, analysis and critique. This trend is not unique to the ELF as it is increasingly common for political movements to utilize the internet as a source of intelligence and training. (Weimann 2006, 123–124)

CONTEXT

The ELF's development was the product of philosophical shifts in the environmental movement, and practical issues that emerged throughout EF! leading to its factionalization. While

---

An Earth Liberation Front Guide. These guides are available on numerous websites and file sharing services.

[24] See for example (Auntie ALF, Uncle ELF and the Anti-Copyright gang 2003, 1–20; Fireant Collective 2001, 1–37; Frontline Information Service n.d., 1998, 8–13; Someone n.d., 1–21)

[25] See for example the guides discussed (109th Congress 2005, 44, 75–76; Anti-Defamation League 2005, 10; Immergut et al. 2007, 134). The two most widely cited arson guides produced by the ELF and ALF respectively are *Setting Fires With Electrical Timers: An Earth Liberation Front Guide* and *Arson-Around with Auntie ALF: Your Guide to Putting Heat on Animal Abusers Everywhere*

[26] It is interesting to note that the referenced ELF and ALF-produced incendiary guides are nearly entirely devoid of ideological or philosophical discussion or even the mention of animal rights. In his discussion of leaderless resistance in the ELF, author Paul Joosse (2007) writes that, "by not explicitly stating ideological precepts, the manual lends itself to use by anyone, regardless of the person's ideological orientation" (2007, 361).

direct action, similarly-styled animal liberation networks such as the BOM and the ALF began in the UK in the early 1970s, the environmental militancy found its focus a bit later. In 1992, following direct actions in England, EF! hosted a national meeting in Brighton. (Leader and Probst 2003, 38) At this meeting, segments of EF! expressed a desire for the movement to halt its use of illegal tactics, and it was decided that as EF!, the movement would refocus on demonstrations, in effect creating the ELF as a new entity to continue producing illegal actions. The ELF name was intentionally chosen because of its similarity to that of the ALF, as the new Earth movement hoped to borrow ALF structure, guidelines and tactics. (Molland 2006, 49)

The emergence of the ELF from EF!'s factionalization allowed it to embrace leadless resistance, while avoiding further ideological splits. It was understood as important to avoid EF!'s mistakes wherein, "factionalization progressed...[and]... energy was diverted towards debates about ideology and away from performing the direct actions...envisioned as being Earth First!'s *forte*" (Joosse 2007, 358). Four years after the ELF emerged in England, it became active in the US, which would quickly become the focal point of the movement's attacks. (Trujillo 2005, 151) On October 31, 1996, the ELF carried out arson, its first major US action after four years of carrying out small vandalisms.[27]

The ELF's emergence was made possible via the broader context of a growing radical environmental movement in Western Europe and North America. (Walton and Widay 2006, 97–99) Thus the emergence of the ELF can be seen as a reactionary movement combating issues such as deforestation and a loss of biodiversity at a time when government policies were seen as disregarding or ignoring the problem. (Ackerman 2003, 155) Following global acknowledgment of such issues, knowledge of GMO agriculture and climate change grew in prominence as well, leading the ELF to execute a number of attacks on GMO crops and research. (Leader and Probst 2003, 46) Similarly, the 1990s saw the emergence of a "sprawl" critique,

---

[27] Between 1992-1996 numerous attacks were carried out that shared tactical and thematic traits with ELF actions. The attacks were carried out in England, Holland, Australia, Germany and New Zealand. (Molland 2006, 52–53)

criticizing the surge in construction of low-density, car-dependent, luxury, urban/suburban housing developments. (Sally and Peter 2006, 415–416) These larger conversations provided the context for an arson campaign targeting luxury home developments, and other large land uses including ski resorts and golf courses. (Ackerman 2003, 153) Following the arson of a "luxury home" under construction[28] an ELF communiqué addressing "sprawl" was released:

> Greetings from the front, The Earth Liberation Front claims responsibility for the torching of a luxury home under construction in Miller Place, Long Island on December 19th. Anti-urban sprawl messages were spraypainted on the walls, then accelerants were poured over the house and lighted...This is the latest in a string of actions in the war against urban sprawl. Urban sprawl not only destroys the green spaces of our planet, but also leads directly to added runoff of pollutants into our waterways, increased traffic that causes congestion and air pollution, and a less pleasing landscape... Unregulated population growth is also a direct product of urban sprawl. There are over 6 billion people on this planet of which almost a third are either starving or living in poverty. Building homes for the wealthy should not even be a priority. (Earth Liberation Front 2000)

The growing global environmental consciousness, with its critique of GMO-technology and sprawl, provided the context for the popularization of radical activism that drew support from the upsurge in complementary leftist movements that occurred in the late 1990s-2000s, following demonstrations opposing the World Trade Organization in Seattle. (Ackerman 2003, 154; starr 2006, 375; Trujillo 2005, 159)

Similarly the anti-globalization initiates of the Zapatista Army for National Liberation (EZLN) in the Mexican state of Chiapas, which peaked in 1994 with the passage of the North American Free Trade Agreement (NAFTA), served to inspire leftist radicals globally as the movement spoke out strongly against Western capitalism and promoted a collective initiate towards environmental protection and sustainability. (Becker 2006, 76–77; Garland 2006, 68)[29]   Within this tradition, the

[28] The arson occurred on December 19, 2000 in Long Island, New York and was claimed via a communiqué sent to the ELF Press Offices.

[29] In at least two ELF communiqués the Zapatista movement was referenced as a source of inspiration. The first, issued in 1997 under the title, "Beltane, 1997" (Best and Nocella, 408-9) and the second, issued on 28 June 1998, and

ELF can be said to be enacting a form of revolutionarily defensive environmentalism advocated by the ELZN. For example, the establishment of the 1978 Montes Azules Biosphere Reserve by Mexican President Jose Lopez Portillo, expropriated 940,000 acres of the Lacandon Jungle from largely indigenous communities, and led to the radicalization and militarization of the EZLN. Self-defense structures were established when the State attempted to move these individuals and in 1989, a ban on wood cutting and the establishment of a State-aligned security force to implement such measures led to one of the first offensive strikes by the EZLN. In this incident in March 1993, EZLN fighters killed two members of the Mexican security forces who had come upon a clandestine sawmill located near the city of San Cristobal. Less than one year later, when the EZLN led a largely bloodless uprising following the passage of NAFTA, one of their first achievements was to expel thousands of oil workers employed by PEMEX, US Western Oil and Geofisica Corporation. For both the ELF and EZLN, the active defense of the ecological realm is not a matter of long-term campaigning, but immediate, reactionary, needs-based maneuvers. Both movements act within the logic of an ever-shortening timeline for appropriate measures and resultantly, shun reformist methods that offer State-involvement, compromised negotiations and further entanglement with the legislative process.

MEMBERSHIP: CLANDESTINE

Establishing membership is a difficult endeavor amongst a movement that does not have members, and as individuals do not *join* the ELF, membership status is tricky to discern. (Helios Global, Inc. 2008, 9) There is a lack of open source material, provided by security services documenting or estimating numbers of ELF cells. (Helios Global, Inc. 2008, 3) The only known ELF members or cells are the relatively few that have been identified and arrested. (Ackerman 2003, 151) NAELFPO (2001) addressed the question, writing that "it is next to impossible to estimate the number of ELF members internationally or even country by country." The closest discernable figures concerning the size of the ELF may come from a 2001 estimate, reporting that the ALF, a similarly structured movement, has an

(available at http://www.elfpressoffice.org/comm062898.swf)

estimated "100 hardcore members" (Helios Global, Inc. 2008, 2). Such a figure appears arbitrary and most likely erroneous. What is known however is that as activity has waned in the US in the latter part of the 2000s, it has resultantly risen in other countries such as Mexico, Russia, the UK and many parts of Western Europe and South America (Loadenthal 2010). Despite the fact that the number of ELF members is unknown, a membership profile exists. From these records, the profile of the most typical ELF activist emerges indicating the individual is likely male, well educated, possessing a high technical capability (Ackerman 2003, 148, 151), under the age of twenty-five, Caucasian, middle to upper-middle-class, from an industrialized Western nation (Helios Global, Inc. 2008, 3), supportive of environmentalism and animal rights (Walton and Widay 2006, 99), active in larger activist movements (Ackerman 2003, 145), and disenfranchised with mainstream environmental protest (Joosse 2007, 356). Sporadic arrests over the last ten years have shown these findings to be generalizable despite the arrest of numerous females and individuals acting in a host of non-Western countries from Indonesia to Bolivia. Recruitment and incitement propaganda produced by ELF-affiliated entities may also consciously attempt to engage youth subcultures through a positive portrayal of the movements as 'instigators of violent action' (Joosse 2007, 360).

This characterization is not surprising as Gary Perlstein (2003) writes that the ELF receives "a great deal of moral and perhaps even financial support from politically liberal urban... [and] academic settings" (2003, 171–172). Thus US universities may be a 'recruitment' setting as many attendees would share demographics characteristics. Thus if a movement seeks to 'recruit' twenty-one year old, privileged, well educated, politically liberal individuals from the industrialized West, the university setting is ideal. This 'supportive' university environment can also be seen in events held on campus supporting radical environmentalism generally, and the ELF specifically. (Helios Global, Inc. 2008, 26; Jarboe 2002) For example, pro-ELF and ALF speakers have given presentations at numerous leftist conferences and gatherings including the National Conference on Organized Resistance, the animal Animal Rights conference, the Liberation Now tour, as well as the Primate Freedom Tour which featured former ELF spokesmen, Craig Rosebraugh. In 1998, Rosenbraugh, and ELF arsonist Jonathan Paul, presented at the National Animal Rights Conference being held at the University of Oregon, urging unity between the ELF and the ALF.

From the available information, the most typical membership in the clandestine elements of the ELF would likely be filled by a Caucasian male between the ages of 18 and 25, from a middle/upper-middle class background, living in the US. He would likely be attending, or have graduated from post-secondary education, identify with anti-authoritarian leftist politics, and be involved in public, aboveground social change movements possibly related to environmentalism, animal rights or anti-globalization. Other indicators such as proficiency with computers or dietary choices may be instructive but are largely anecdotal.

MEMBERSHIP: ABOVEGROUND

Membership in the ELF is not limited to clandestine cells. A multinational, aboveground support structure exists to disseminate propaganda, support prisoners, publicize actions, provide legal support, and allow pro-ELF persons a venue to promote the aims of radical environmentalism. At present, there exists a host of explicitly pro-ELF print and online magazines in national distribution throughout the US. Two examples are *Bite Back* magazine,[30] (in print 2001-present) and *No Compromise* magazine,[31] (in print 1989-2006). Both magazines focus on the ac-

---

[30] *Bite Back magazine* is published irregularly since 2001 and available at: http://www.directaction.info/

[31] *No Compromise* is published biannually since 1989. According to the *No Compromise magazine* website, the publication is "the militant, direct action publication of grassroots animal liberationists and their supporters," with the aim of "unifying grassroots animal liberationists by providing a forum where activists can exchange information, share strategy, discuss important issues within the movement, network with each other in an open and respectful environment and strengthen the grassroots." Website available at: http://www.nocompromise.org/ with a full archive made available at http://thetalonconspiracy.com/category/periodicals/nocomp/

tions of the ALF but also provide coverage of ELF attacks and prisoners.

Bite Back and *No Compromise* deal primarily with the ALF, addressing the ELF as a supportive ally, but in 2009, an explicitly pro-ELF magazine was created entitled *Resistance: Journal of the Earth Liberation Movement*. Currently in its third issue, *Resistance* (2009) plans to publish four issues a year with the stated goal of providing "a vehicle to inform, inspire, and energize the earth liberation movement." Although *Resistance* appears to be a project independent of the NAELFPO, its former spokesmen Craig Rosebraugh, is the founder of Arissa Media Group which is the journal's distributor. (Arissa Media Group 2009) Both *Resistance* and Arissa unequivocally embrace the ELF publicly, whereas *Bite Back* and *No Compromise* share tactical methods and a broad affinity. Additionally, there is *The Earth First! Journal* published since the early 1980s and often covering attacks associated with the ELF and other clandestine, pro-environment groups. Currently the *EF! Journal* is published six times a year containing:

> ...reports on direct action; articles on the preservation of wilderness and biological diversity; news and announcements about EF! and other radical environmental groups; investigative articles; critiques of the entire environmental movement...essays exploring ecological theory...(*Earth First! Journal* 2009)

The journal's creators describe the periodical as "The voice of the radical environmental movement...[and] an essential forum for discussion" (2009) within the radical environmentalist movement.

Beyond these supporters there exist numerous periodicals that regularly praise radical environmentalism and green anarchism, often documenting ELF attacks. Examples published in the US include *Green Anarchy*,[32] (in print 1999-2008), *Fifth Estate*,[33] (in print 1965-present), and *Species Traitor*[34] (in print 2000-2005). In total, there are more than eight periodicals, reg-

---

[32] The complete title is *Green Anarchy: an anti-civilization journal of theory & action*. The magazine is published bi-annually since 1999. The *Green Anarchy* website is available at: http://greenanarchy.org/

[33] The complete title is *Fifth Estate: an anti-authoritarian magazine of ideas & action*. The magazine is published quarterly since 1965. The *Fifth Estate* website is available at: http://www.fifthestate.org/

ularly published in the US that document and promote the ELF and sympathetically publicize ELF-affiliated prisoners, in effect allowing these organizations to act as an aboveground support networks facilitating the building and maintenance of a pro-ELF movement.

The aboveground support networks of the ELF extend beyond publications, and provide support to individuals arrested and imprisoned for attacks. This prisoner support network identifies and tracks ELF-affiliated prisoners around the world. (Anti-Defamation League 2005, 11; Helios Global, Inc. 2008, 26) This information allows supporters to learn about prisoners, and write letters to those incarcerated, broadening the public support network to peripheral, sympathetic individuals. At least four organizations are currently operating to meet the needs of ELF prisoners[35] Additional aboveground support networks for the ELF include the North American Earth Liberation Front Press Office (currently offline) which anonymously receives ELF communiqués from cells and publicizes them globally. Though currently the NAELFPO has no aboveground individual speaking on its behalf, in the past both Craig Rosenbraugh and Leslie James Pickering served as official spokesmen for the ELF through its Press Office. Rosenbraugh and Pickering have also both authored books documenting the ELF.[36] Furthermore, Rosenbraugh's project, Arissa Media group (now managed by the Institute for Critical Animal Studies and not Rosenbraugh) distributes books, magazines and CDs promoting the ELF. In 2008, the National Lawyers Guild, established the "Green Scare hotline," in response to a series of

---

[34] *Species Traitor* is published irregularly since 2000 and has no website at present.

[35] The English language prisoner support groups which specifically track ELF-affiliated prisoners include the North American Earth Liberation Prisoners Support Network (http://www.ecoprisoners.org), the Anarchist Black Cross Federation (http://www.abcf.net) and the currently offline Earth Liberation Prisoners Support Network (http://www.spiritoffreedom.org.uk).

[36] In 2003, as part of a Master's thesis, Craig Rosebraugh wrote *The Logic of Political Violence: Lessons in Reform and Revolution* and later, in 2004 he wrote *Burning Rage of a Dying Planet: Speaking for the Earth Liberation Front*. In 2006 Leslie James Pickering wrote *Earth Liberation Front 1997-2002* and has also written articles in the newly formed, pro-ELF magazine Resistance.

arrests targeting ELF cells. The purpose of the hotline is to provide support to individuals arrested or accused of involvement with environmental or animal rights motivated attacks. The hotline will assist the individual in locating a lawyer. The Guild has also published a guide, entitled *Operation Backfire: A Survival Guide for Environmental and Animal Rights Activists* (2009), explaining activists' legal rights and anti-terrorism laws as they have been applied in prosecutions of ELF-ALF members.

The functions of aboveground support entities are crucial for clandestine members to function effectively. The separation allows cells to remain unseen and unheard while supporters act as their voice and promoters. In this model, the cells carry out attacks, and the supporters document and disseminate propaganda the movement creates but is not able to distribute for fear of discovery. (Joosse 2007, 353) Under this model, based on the leaderless resistance structure, both the clandestine and public actors are necessary participants as both operate within complementary spheres of involvement predicated on a shared ideology and divergent tactics.

CONCLUSION: NEO-GUERILLAS & NEW SOCIAL MOVEMENTS

The ELF is a network of clandestine, autonomous cells, organized via a decentralized and broad ideology based in deep ecology, primitivist-themed anarchism, collective defense of the natural world, and a critique of environmental policy, genetic engineering, residential development, and globalized capitalism. The success of ELF cells avoiding discovery and arrest has limited the available data concerning the identity of participants, but a broad profile does exist as it pertains to sex, race, age, class, nationality, political affiliation and education. The ELF network emerged as support grew for the use of illegal protest tactics within the British radical environmental movement, modeling itself after the ALF as a leaderless resistance movement choosing sabotage, arson and vandalism as its main tactics. These attacks are carried out by tactically proficient, highly secure, small unit cells, using easily accessible weapons technologies and online instruction. This underground network of attackers is aided by aboveground support structures which help to promote and publicize the aims of the clandestine units.

The popularity and deterritorialization of the ELF in the US has served as a tactical and strategic inspiration to a host of movements who have drawn from the ELF's methods for a variety of goals. In this sense, the ELF, despite its decline in domestic activity, must be understood as an instrumental social movement in the post-millennial period of radical, direct action, anti-State politics. Its praxis of insurrectionary-styled direct attack and unmediated offensive strikes offers inspiration to activists; inspiration which is aided by the network's relative imperviousness to disruption, arrest and infiltration. Despite being established as a 'number one domestic terrorist threat' by the US intelligence community, and despite malicious prosecutions and egregious sentencing of activists, the network remains.

Since around 2007 when to so-called anti-globalization, counter-summit movement declined in the US, a large number of activists were left with a time vacuum. Hours that had once been dedicated to planning outreach, recruitment, logistical preparation and infrastructure building (e.g. housing, food, legal support networks) were now freed. While it is too early to make such determinations, it is entirely possible that with the decline of such mass-based protest movements, some individuals shifted their *modus operandi* towards what the military would term 'small unit tactics.' In other words, when regional and national mobilizations proved to be a resource-intensive, short victory producing avenue of resistance, attack histories such as that of the ELF may have led the charge for a multitude of movements to embrace lone wolf, leaderless resistance and urban guerilla tactics which had declined in domestic popularity with the disbanding of the United Freedom Front, George Jackson Brigade, Black Liberation Army (BLA), May 19th Communist Organization and others in the 1980s. Just as the decline of the anti-Viet Nam revolutionary groups (e.g. Weather Underground, Black Panthers) led to the establishment of the more vanguardist 'Peoples Armies' such as the BLA, so too may have the latter's decline left a void filled by the rise of clandestine property destruction networks in the early 1990s. In this sense, the ELF should be understood historically as an instrumental tactical and strategic tendency in North American protest as it offered a model of outright resistance at a time when aboveground movements were gaining publicity and momentum.

At present, in 2013, the North American environmental justice movement is once again experiencing a period of growth and diversification. Popular movements utilizing non-violence civil disobedience are prominent in their position of the transnational Keystone Pipeline for transporting oil and the more generalized use of hydraulic fracturing (often called hydrofracking) for extracting natural gas and petroleum from subterranean areas. Continued logging campaigns in the Pacific Northwest has led to the reinvigoration of forest defense and encampment campaigns such as those being fought by Cascadia Forest Defenders. These movements, while adopting self-sacrificial civil disobedience (e.g. lockdowns, tree sits, tripods) as their main tactics, will also likely include the use of clandestine, ELF-inspired property destruction. Previous campaigns around the world have witnessed such a hybridized campaign, often with great success. To cite but one example, in 2010, activists in Scotland were able to derail the construction of numerous open cast coalmines (i.e. strip mines) through the use of forest defense in conjunction with the anonymous sabotage of machinery at sites like the Mainshill Solidarity Camp. The company building and managing the mines, Scottish Coal, financially collapsed in early 2013, likely pushed into ruin by the costly and frequently sabotages it experienced during the anti-open cast campaign. Following one particularly costly construction equipment sabotage by anonymous monkey wrenches, the activists released this statement to Scotland's *Indymedia*:

> In the early hours of this morning machinery at Mainshill open cast site was sabotaged. Two Caterpillar D9T's and a 170 tonne face scrapping earth mover, an O&K RH90, were targeted, both will be inoperable today, and will cost Scottish Coal greatly...The machinery at the Mainshill site, and any other coal site in Scotland, are extremely vulnerable. Sabotage against the coal industry will continue until its expansion is halted. This action was done by autonomous environmentalists in solidarity with the people of South Lanarkshire [Scotland] who are fighting to save their community and their health from the coal industry. This is also in solidarity with people around the world, including Columbia and India, who are fighting for their lives against the coal industry. (Anonymous 2010)

From this short communication one can see broad affinity with the ELF in its methods as well as its politics. The use of clandestine sabotage in defense of the Earth did not begin nor end with the ELF, but the network has been key in the invigoration of a sense of possible victory. The production of spectacular, multimillion-dollar strikes time and again has had a catalyzing effect on those that stand in the shadow of foreboding multinational giants such as Monsanto, Exxon and the likes.

Since the US made its largest arrests during Operation Backfire in 2005, it touted the end of the ELF with 'key' members in custody and jailed. Despite this great loss to the movement, the international growth of the ELF since that time has been remarkable. What started as a small attack tendency in mid-90s Oregon is now a history of ELF-claimed attacks in a host of countries including Australia, Canada, Chile, Colombia, Iceland, Indonesia, Italy, Mexico, Netherlands, New Zealand, Russia, Sweden and the UK. In the past two years in particular the ELF name has been partnered in numerous attacks claimed by the Informal Anarchist Federation (FAI) and the International Revolutionary Front (IRF) in attacks throughout Europe, Asia and the Americas.

The ELF is not an organization in the traditional sense and is more akin to a movement of informal networks. Names such as the ELF, ALF, EF!, FIA, IRF are freely adoptable political markers providing little more than an articulation of a shared politic and recognizable name. The usage of such names to claim attacks allows disparate actors to present themselves as a global movement, linking isolated cells and individuals through a central meaning. Thus, the adoption of the ELF moniker in conjunction with newly established clandestine attack networks such as the FAI and IRF speaks to the draw of the ELF as an *idea* more than a collectivity of individuals or single, isolated actions. In the end, the ELF may die as a domestic network and live on as an idea—an idea to be included in the signatory line of communiqués claiming responsibility for attacks in perpetuity, serving to carry the ELF moniker far beyond its original horizons and into the annuls of radical history.

REFERENCES

109th Congress. 2005. "Oversight on Eco-Terrorism Specifically Examining the Earth Liberation Front ('ELF') and the Animal Liberation Front ('ALF')." http://epw.senate.gov/hearing_statements.cfm?id=237836 (April 2, 2012).

Ackerman, Gary A. 2003. "Beyond Arson? a Threat Assessment of the Earth Liberation Front." *Terrorism and Political Violence* 15(4): 143–70.

Anonymous. 2010. "Mainshill Coal Site Sabotage!" http://www.indymediascotland.org/node/18959 (January 1, 2013).

Anti-Defamation League. 2005. "Ecoterrorism: Extremism in the Animal Right and Environmentalist Movements." http://www.adl.org/learn/ext_us/Ecoterrorism_print.asp (January 1, 2013).

Arissa Media Group. 2009. "About - Arissa Media Group, LLC." *Resistance Magazine*. http://www.arissa.org/about.html (December 20, 2009).

Auntie ALF, Uncle ELF and the Anti-Copyright gang. 2003. "Arson Around with Auntie ALF: Your Guide for Putting the Heat on Animal Abusers Everywhere." http://archive.org/stream/ArsonaroundWithAuntieAlf#page/n0/mode/2up (January 1, 2013).

Beam, Louis. 1992. "Leaderless Resistance." *The Seditionist* (12). http://www.louisbeam.com/leaderless.htm (January 1, 2013).

Becker, Michael. 2006. "Ontological Anarchism: The Philosophical Roots of Revolutionary Environmentalism." In *Igniting a Revolution: Voices in Defense of the Earth*, eds. Steven Best and Anthony Nocella. Oakland, CA: AK Press.

Borum, Randy, and Chuck Tilby. 2005. "Anarchist Direct Actions: A Challenge for Law Enforcement." *Studies in Conflict & Terrorism* 28(3): 201–23.

Chalk, Peter. 2001. "U.S. Environmental Groups and 'Leaderless Resistance'." *Jane's Intelligence Review [republished by RAND Corporation]*. http://www.rand.org/commentary/2001/07/01/JIR.html (January 1, 2013).

Dishman, Chris. 2005. "The Leaderless Nexus: When Crime and Terror Converge." *Studies in Conflict & Terrorism* 28(3): 237–52.

Eagan, Sean P. 1996. "From Spikes to Bombs: The Rise of Eco-terrorism." *Studies in Conflict & Terrorism* 19(1): 1–18.

Earth First! Journal. 2009. "About the Earth First! Journal." *Earth First! Journal*. http://www.earthfirstjournal.org/subsection.php?id=5>. (December 20, 2009).

Earth Liberation Front. 2000. "Communiqué - 12.19.00." http://www.elfpressoffice.org/comm121900.html (December 20, 2009).

FBI Counterterrorism and Cyber Divisions. 2004. "Tactics Used by Eco-Terrorists to Detect and Thwart Law Enforcement Operations."

Fireant Collective. 2001. "Setting Fires With Electrical Timers: An Earth Liberation Front Guide." http://www.scribd.com/doc/10523512/Setting-Fires-With-Electrical-Timers (January 1, 2013).

Frontline Information Service. n.d. "A Final Nail Exclusive: Electronically Timed Incendiary Igniter." http://www.animalliberation.net/finalnail/index.html.

———. 1998. "The Final Nail: Destroying the Fur Industry - A Guided Tour #2." http://www.animalliberation.net/finalnail/index.html.

Garland, Davey. 2006. "To Cast a Giant Shadow: Revolutionary Ecology and Its Practical Implementation Through the Earth Liberation Front." In *Igniting a Revolution: Voices in Defense of the Earth*, eds. Steven Best and Anthony Nocella. Oakland, CA: AK Press.

Helios Global, Inc. 2008. "Ecoterrorism: Environmental and Animal-Rights Militants in the United States."

Immergut, Karin J., Kirk A. Engdall, Stephen F. Peifer, and John C. Ray. 2007. "Government's Sentencing Memorandum in the United States District Court for the District of Oregon [case Numbers CR 06-60069-AA, CR 06-60070-AA, CR 06-60071-AA, CR 06-60078-AA, CR 06-60079-AA, CR 06-60080-AA, CR 06-60120-AA, 06-60122-AA, 06-60123-AA, 06-60124-AA, 06-60125-AA, 06-60126-AA]."

Jackson, Brian, and David Frelinger. 2008. "Rifling Through the Terrorists' Arsenal: Exploring Groups' Weapon Choices and Technology Strategies." *Studies in Conflict & Terrorism* 31(7). http://www.rand.org/pubs/working_papers/WR533. (December 12, 2012).

Jarboe, James. 2002. "The Threat of Eco-Terrorism." http://www.fbi.gov/news/testimony/the-threat-of-eco-terrorism (April 4, 2012).

jones, pattrice. 2006. "Stomping with the Elephants: Feminist Principles for Radical Solidarity." In *Igniting a Revolution: Voices in Defense of the Earth*, eds. Steven Best and Anthony Nocella. Oakland, CA: AK Press.

Joosse, Paul. 2007. "Leaderless Resistance and Ideological Inclusion: The Case of the Earth Liberation Front." *Terrorism and Political Violence* 19(3): 351–68.

Laqueur, Walter. 2000. *The New Terrorism: Fanaticism and the Arms of Mass Destruction*. Oxford University Press, USA.

Leader, Stefan H., and Peter Probst. 2003. "The Earth Liberation Front And Environmental Terrorism." *Terrorism and Political Violence* 15(4): 37–58.

Lewis, John. 2004. "Animal Rights Extremism and Ecoterrorism." http://www.fbi.gov/news/testimony/animal-rights-extremism-and-ecoterrorism (April 5, 2012).

Loadenthal, Michael. 2010. "Nor Hostages, Assassinations, or Hijackings, but Sabotage, Vandalism & Fire: 'Eco-Terrorism' as Political Violence

Challenging the State and Capital." MLitt Dissertation. Centre for the
Study of Terrorism and Political Violence, University of St Andrews.

————. 2012. "Operation Splash Back!: Queering Animal Liberation
Through the Contributions of Neo-Insurrectionist Queers." *Journal of
Critical Animal Studies* Special Edition: Intersecting Queer Theory and
Critical Animal Studies.

————. 2013. "Deconstructing 'eco-terrorism': Rhetoric, Framing and
Statecraft as Seen through the Insight Approach." *Critical Studies on
Terrorism* 6(1).
http://www.tandfonline.com/doi/abs/10.1080/17539153.2013.765702.

Lovitz, Dara. 2010. *Muzzling a Movement: The Effects of Anti-Terrorism
Law, Money, and Politics on Animal Activism.* Lantern Books.

Molland, Noel. 2006. "A Spark That Ignited a Flame: The Evolution of the
Earth Liberation Front." In *Igniting a Revolution: Voices in Defense of
the Earth*, eds. Steven Best and Anthony Nocella. Oakland, CA: AK
Press, 47–58.

Nacos, Brigitte. 2006. "Communication and Recruitment of Terrorists." In
*The Making of a Terrorist Volume 1: Recruitment, Training, and Root
Causes*, The Making of a Terrorist, ed. James J. F. Forest. Westport:
Praeger Security International.

National Lawyers Guild. 2009. "Operation Backfire: A Survival Guide for
Environmental and Animal Rights Activists."
http://www.nlg.org/resource/know-your-rights/operation-backfire
(January 1, 2013).

North American Earth Liberation Front Press Office. 2001. "Frequently
Asked Questions About the Earth Liberation Front."
http://www.elfpressoffice.org/elffaqs.html (December 18, 2009).

————. 2009a. "Earth Liberation Front Diary of Actions- 1999."
http://www.elfpressoffice.org/actions1999.html (January 10, 2010).

————. 2009b. "Earth Liberation Front Diary of Actions- 2003."
http://www.elfpressoffice.org/actions2003.html (January 10, 2010).

————. 2009c. "Earth Liberation Front Diary of Actions- 2006."
http://www.elfpressoffice.org/actions2006.html (January 10, 2010).

Perlstein, Gary. 2003. "Comments on Ackerman." *Terrorism and Political
Violence* 15(4): 171–72.

Potter, Will. 2011. *Green Is the New Red: An Insider's Account of a Social
Movement Under Siege.* 1st ed. City Lights Publishers.

Resistance Magazine. 2009. "About - Resistance: Journal of the Earth
Liberation Movement." *Resistance Magazine.*
http://www.resistancemagazine.org/about.html (December 20, 2009).

Sally and Peter. 2006. "ELF Claims Vandalism Against New Housing
Developments in Philadelphia Suburb." In *Igniting a Revolution: Voices*

in Defense of the Earth, eds. Steven Best and Anthony Nocella. Oakland, CA: AK Press, 415–16.

Schuster, Henry. 2005. "Domestic Terror: Who's Most Dangerous?" *CNN.* http://www.cnn.com/2005/US/08/24/schuster.column/index.html>. (November 10, 2010).

Slater, Colin. 2011. "Activism as Terrorism: The Green Scare, Radical Environmentalism and Govermentality." *Anarchist Developments in Cultural Studies* (Ten Years After 9/11: An Anarchist Evaluation): 211– 38.

Someone. n.d. "The Animal Liberation Primer [3rd Ed.]." http://www.animalliberationfront.com/ALFront/primer3.pdf (January 1, 2013).

starr, amory. 2006. "Grumpywarriorcool: What Makes Our Movements White." In *Igniting a Revolution: Voices in Defense of the Earth*, eds. Steven Best and Anthony Nocella. Oakland, CA: AK Press.

Taylor, Bron. 1998. "Religion, Violence and Radical Environmentalism: From Earth First! to the Unabomber to the Earth Liberation Front." *Terrorism and Political Violence* 10(4): 1–42.

————. 2003. "Threat Assessments and Radical Environmentalism." *Terrorism and Political Violence* 15(4): 173–82.

The Green Anarchy Collective. 2009. "Back to Basics Vol. #4 - What Is Green Anarchy: 'An Introduction to Anti-Civilization Anarchist Thought and Practice'." http://www.greenanarchy.org/index.php? action=viewwritingdetail&writingId=283 (December 18, 2009).

Trujillo, Horacio. 2005. "Chapter 6: The Radical Environmentalist Movement." In *Aptitude for Destruction: Case Studies of Organizational Learning in Five Terrorist Groups*, Arlington, VA: RAND Corporation.

Walton, Matthew, and Jessica Widay. 2006. "Shades of Green: Examining Cooperation Between Radical and Mainstream Environmentalists." In *Igniting a Revolution: Voices in Defense of the Earth*, eds. Steven Best and Anthony Nocella. Oakland, CA: AK Press, 415–16.

Weimann, Gabriel. 2006. *Terror on the Internet: The New Arena, the New Challenges.* 1st ed. United States Institute of Peace Press.

Yin, Robert K. 2008. *Case Study Research: Design and Methods.* 4th ed. SAGE Publications, Inc.

Fighting Inequality in Hong Kong: Lessons Learned from Occupy Hong Kong

ANGIE NG[1]

This article provides an analysis of Occupy Hong Kong, the socioeconomic conditions of its emergence, and mainstream media responses to the movement. It gives an overview of the situation of inequality in Hong Kong, from a progressive perspective, using direct ethnographic data supplemented by official numbers, as this situation of inequality is what gave rise to the local manifestation of the Occupy spirit. The article also examines how the local Occupy movement was portrayed by the *South China Morning Post*, as part of a local press known to minimize inequality as an issue and act as an agent of social control. The paper also describes the lessons to be learned from Occupy Hong Kong and its strategy, especially in relation to the press. Before this, the international Occupy movement, Occupy Hong Kong and the local context are briefly discussed.

THE INTERNATIONAL OCCUPY MOVEMENT

The international Occupy movement started with the Occupation in New York City on 17 September 2011 (Chomsky 2012) and quickly spread around the world. The movement was in-

[1] Angie Ng is a PhD student in Applied Social Sciences at Durham University (U.K.). Her research interests include trafficking in women, violence against women, general health and social movements and the media. She can be reached at: angie.ng@durham.ac.uk

The author would like to thank the peer reviewer and editors at Radical Criminology for their time and constructive comments. She would also like to express her appreciation to all those involved in the Occupy movement in Hong Kong.

spired by, amongst other events, the revolutions in Tunisia and Egypt (Dean 2011) and can also be seen as part of the mobilization against corporate globalization and resulting inequalities that have been increasing for more than ten years (Smith 2011). The USA was becoming increasingly similar to Huxley's *Brave New World*, with the people doing all the work being lulled into complacency with distractions and advertisement by big business. (*ibid*). At a time when conservative policies were presented under the banner of personal freedom or responsibility, the Occupy movement brought issues of inequality and social justice from the margins of public discourse into the centre of it (Varon 2012; Schossboeck 2012). Instead of continuing belief in the "trickle down effect," the Occupation claimed there was a division between the 99% and the 1% and declared that division to be one of exploitation (Dean 2011); it has provoked some changes in attitudes and beliefs (Schossboeck 2012).

On 17 September, 2,000 people occupied Zuccotti Park with the message that the 99% of the world's population would no longer put up with the greed and corruption of the 1%, protesting the unregulated financial speculation that caused the global financial crisis and fighting for a world based on human need and sustainability instead of thirst for profits (Goodman and Moynihan 2012). Seeing the rising income disparity, nationally and globally, the people realised they had been abandoned by a political system that creates more wealth for the already wealthy at the expense of the regular people using the processes of precaritization and austerity, slowly adjusting the people to insecurity and hopelessness as jobs become temporary, social services are cut down and social democracy is replaced by ideologies of personal responsibility (Butler 2011).

According to Chomsky (2012), this movement was the first major popular reaction to a three-decade-long class war and also the first major public response that could reverse the trend in increasing inequality. This decades-long class war had resulted in the top 1% in the USA seeing an income increase of 275% while almost everyone else saw a yearly income rise of only about 1%. The bodies assembled together in Occupy expressed the message that they are not disposable; they called for a livable wage and demanded justice (Butler 2011), and a fundamental change in the way the socio-economic and political institutions are ordered (*ibid*). Meanwhile, the mainstream press first ignored and then twisted the voices of Occupiers, as part of a mass culture that sells its construction of society to regular people, while shaping public opinion and protecting the 1% (Davidson 2012).

Despite a lack of national or regional coordination (Varon 2012), the movement spread around the world. Being part of a global movement allowed everyone to resist together, and in so doing, realise they are suffering together and so they began to display the social bond of solidarity that neoliberalism is trying to destroy (Butler 2011).

OCCUPY HONG KONG

As part of the international Occupy movement, Occupy Central, which is also known as Occupy Hong Kong, was mainly initiated by Left21, a group of progressive individuals with an online platform and study group. In brief, Hong Kong as a territory has a government which is closely linked to big business, particularly in finance, real estate and transportation; as such, policies and laws are geared towards increasing wealth and profits for capitalists while politically and economically oppressing workers (which are the large majority) and destroying the environment (InMediaHK 2011). One local goal of Occupiers was to change the way the government worked so that there would be more economic and political equality in Hong Kong (*ibid*); another major purpose was to reflect on the capitalist system, discuss the feasibility of hyper-capitalism and explore alternative systems that could potentially replace it, knowing that without a revolution in the way people think, no revolution would ever succeed, at least not along the correct path (Lam 2011). Other grassroots organizations were contacted and involved, including FM101, Hong Kong's independent, illegal radio station. FM101 was initiated in an environment in which only two companies, Metro Radio and Commercial Radio, control local, non-governmental radio (DeWolf 2010), and FM101 were very much involved in the Occupation. The Occupation began by holding a rally in Exchange Square on 15 October 2011, and then moving to a more "permanent" space underneath the headquarters of HSBC, in the ground-floor, open-air plaza which usually serves as a walkway, at the heart of Hong

Kong's financial district. The camp remained there until members were forcibly evicted on 11 September 2012.

LOCAL CONTEXT

The story of British colonial Hong Kong started with free trade. The Opium War was fought against China under the banner of "free trade", and after China lost this war in 1841, it conceded Hong Kong to Britain (Ropp 2010). In 1997, Hong Kong was returned to China and guaranteed autonomy for 50 years as a Special Administrative Region. Within the list of states the United Nations Development Programme (UNDP) considers as having very high human development, Hong Kong's income disparity comes first, making it even higher than the United States' infamous levels (Einhorn 2009); in fact, the territory has a GINI coefficient[2] of 53.3, ranking fourteen places worse than China, which has a GINI of 48.0, on the global list (CIA 2013) Neoliberal globalization has left there, as in other places, a superfluous population suffering from lack of income security (Chomsky 2012).

Beneath the glitzy facade of one of neoliberalism's poster children, Hong Kong, lies the wage slavery of millions and levels of poverty even more unacceptable in a highly-developed territory. Despite the economic growth Hong Kong has experienced since the 1970s, a high level of economic inequality has continued to plague the city, and this inequality is growing (Chui, Leung and Yip 2012).

Even though Hong Kong is one of the most expensive places in the world in which to live and is experiencing a surge in real-estate prices (*ibid*), over 50 percent of the population earn less than 11,000 Hong Kong Dollars (HKD) per month (BBC News, 2012, as cited by Chui, Leung and Yip 2012), which is roughly 1,419.34 US Dollars per month.

Unlike others OECD countries, which have faced the financial crisis and European debt crisis, for the past ten years, Hong Kong has continued to experience an economic boom (*ibid*); China and other emerging economies have maintained high lev-

---

[2] The **Gini coefficient** (also known as the **Gini index** or **Gini ratio**) is a measure of statistical dispersion, commonly used a way to measure the inequality of income or wealth. (Wikipedia)

els of growth despite the global situation (Drysdale 2012). Despite this, from 2001 to 2010, the income of those in the top 10 percent rose 60 percent while the income of those in the bottom 10 percent not only did not increase at all but decreased by 20 percent (Chen 2012); indeed, employers have been known to use any excuse to cut pay instead of sharing the prosperity with workers (Chui, Leung and Yip 2012). So worker insecurity has increased, in accordance with Alan Greenspan's advice that this precarious existence leads to a healthy economy since their financial insecurity will keep workers from making demands for higher wages (Chomsky 2012). At the same time, housing, education, hospitals, social services, and care for those with special needs have all been falling in standards (Henrard 2012).

CAUSES OF INCOME DISPARITY IN HONG KONG

The large income disparity in Hong Kong stems from different factors, including the following: de-industrialization resulting in a large labor force with low educational levels; monopolism (Chui, Leung and Yip 2012) or plutocracy; low taxation and the lack of government action; property speculation; and an aging population coupled with drops in household size (Henrard 2012). Before discussing public awareness, the following four paragraphs will briefly touch upon these causes of income disparity.

Hong Kong has experienced the same de-industrialization as the US. In the US, companies looking to increase profits in manufacturing shifted jobs abroad, and there was a reverse of the previous trend, that of progress towards industrialization (Chomsky, 2012). The economy shifted from one of productive enterprise to financial manipulation, leading to a concentration of wealth in the financial sector (*ibid*); this in turn led to a concentration of political power, which produced legislation that only accelerated this cycle (*ibid*). Hong Kong is what is known as an oligarchy.

Power is becoming increasingly concentrated in the hands of fewer and fewer financially privileged people. Just as in the US, the population of Hong Kong living a precarious existence is no longer confined to the fringes of society (Chomsky 2012); last year, out of 2.8 million workers there were 180,600 workers (or 6.4%) earning less than the minimum wage, and inclusive of these, 895,500 workers (31.9%) earned under 40 HKD per hour[3] (Census and Statistics Department, 2012: 55). While the working- and middle-class people have gotten by via artificial means, including longer working hours and high rates of borrowing as in the US (Chomsky 2012), wealth has become concentrated in the hands of fewer and fewer people, leading to these few privileged people having power over the working class and poor people. In such a situation, it is apparent that government policies are not making Hong Kong a more egalitarian place.

Unlike other OECD countries, which are in debt, Hong Kong has a yearly budget surplus of $71.3 billion HKD (Henrard 2012). Despite this, public spending on social policy issues is relatively low in this territory as the government prefers to encourage people to work (*ibid*). Indeed, Hong Kong is known as a low-tax economy (*ibid*) and poster child for neoliberalism and laissez-faire economics.

Along the same lines, there is little incentive for more long-term, concrete action to alleviate the housing crisis. Hyper-gentrification is taking place in all areas of Hong Kong, with luxury developments cropping up everywhere, leading Hong Kong's median home price to be 12.6 times the annual median income (Demographia 2012); in comparison, the figures for the United States and Canada are just 3.0 and 3.5 respectively (*ibid*). While speculators and real-estate developers have been raking in large profits, the city has in recent years become notorious around the world for having cage homes, which are coffin-sized cages stacked on top of each other with many to a room (Chen 2012).

With the elderly making up more than forty percent of recipients of social security (Fisher 2012), many of the occupants of these cage homes are elderly people. Due to Hong Kong's lack of a sustainable retirement protection scheme or pension plan for its people, poverty is a risk of old age here (*ibid*).

---

[3] 40 HKD = ~ $5 USD / CAN (As of July, 2013)

Public Awareness

Meanwhile, the author found, through participant observation and interviews with people involved, that the general spirit of the people here is similar to that in the US, as described by Chomsky (2012). Older participants interviewed reported that people in general used to understand they had civic responsibilities, but this has been replaced by rampant individualism. In order to control the population and ensure minimal disturbance to their rule, the dominant class has used public relations to lead society to become increasingly consumeristic, distracted by entertainment news and the like, passive and apathetic.

Despite this, public awareness on the issue of inequality has been spreading across Hong Kong, leading to social discontent (Henrard 2012) and social instability (Chui, Leung and Yip 2012). In response to this growing general dissatisfaction, the government initiated "Scheme $6,000", handing out 6000 HKD[4] to each person who both qualified as a permanent resident and reached the age of 18 before 31 Mar 2012 (Scheme6000 2012); a variety of other one-off relief efforts for the deprived have also been carried out (Henrard 2012). The government also implemented its first minimum hourly wage in 2011, with the minimum wage set at 28 HKD per hour[5] (Henrard 2012). There is also a new, old-age living allowance scheme (Fisher 2012). However, there is a need for long-term social policies (Henrard 2012), not just temporary solutions.

Methods

This research work uses ethnography, including participant observation and informal interviews. The data was originally collected as part of the author's PhD research conducted on a separate topic in the territory. As a supporter, the author attended the inaugural event that started the Occupation in Hong Kong, visited frequently and witnessed various changes in the movement. She also had the opportunity to speak to various members, regular citizens and others in civil society, such as members of local NGOs.

---

[4] Approximately $774 USD

[5] ~ $3.60 USD

This research also uses a thematic analysis of English-language news articles from the top-rated local paper, the South China Morning Post (SCMP), which also happens to be targeted at expatriates and higher-income individuals. The articles analyzed were published during the period of 1 October to 31 October 2011, which includes the fifteen days before and the fifteen days after the first day of the Occupation in Hong Kong and 27 August - 26 September 2012, which include the fifteen days before and the fifteen days after Occupy was evicted.

FINDINGS AND DISCUSSION:
INEQUALITY IN HONG KONG

The lack of affordable dwellings is a pressing concern for people in Hong Kong, mentioned by informants, presented as a major social justice issue in protests and brought up even in the mainstream media; for example, a collection of photos is available from the newspaper, *Tai Kung Pao* (Lau 2012), and 2012's Hong Kong Artwalk featured an exhibit named "Sojourning as tempura - Inadequate Housing Photo Exhibition" (Society for Community Organisation 2012). Due to the high profile nature of this social issue, it has become common knowledge that whole families sometimes live in squalid rooms, and different people live in cage/coffin homes; these places can exist in the same neighborhoods as luxury developments, which have cropped up even in low-income areas. Many adults can barely financially provide for themselves and any children they may have, let alone their elderly parents. As a result, many old folks, along with other vulnerable people, live in cage/coffin homes; with rents for these spaces being around 3000 HKD a month, as reported by informants and seen in Lau (2012: 18), many people have to work as rag pickers or janitors during the day in order to have a cage home to sleep in at night. Rag pickers, such as an elderly lady the author spoke with in Shum Shui Po, can receive 10 HKD for a trolley full of cardboard, and sometimes, they trade their found recyclables for rolls of toilet paper or other daily necessities instead.

A local informant conveyed to the author that many of these older people living in poverty bought into the dream that education would raise their children out of poverty, and through hard-earned life savings, and even borrowing from loan sharks, they put their children in college just to find out that there was no living-wage available. These elderly people are losing hope and express feelings of great despair. This echoes Chomsky's (2012) observation of the American people; where there used to be a sense of hope in the future, now there is just a sense of despair (*ibid*).

Meanwhile, the large shopping centers and businesses are strangling small businesses, not only obliging the general population to buy from their over-priced venues, but also forcing workers and owners to lose their livelihoods. According to one informant in social work, in response to the overpricing of commodities, there are illegal market places in which the poor can buy, for example, half-used bottles of soy sauce and other used items. This informant and others mentioned that some elderly people have been forced to go through garbage cans to find scraps of food to eat, and others have been pressed to steal food from street vendors just in order to prevent starvation; when the author witnessed an elderly man caught stealing fruit, the owner of an adjacent stall mentioned to her that the elderly man was so pitiful and the situation occurs "all the time."

As a result of the general loss of livelihoods, there is a desperately vulnerable supply of extremely low-cost labor. The minimum wage, which only came into effect in 2011, is currently 28 HKD per hour (Henrard, 2012). Just to illustrate, in order to rent a coffin/cage home alone, one of these workers would have to work over 100 hours per month. As if 28 HKD per hour is not a low enough wage, some job seekers are forced to take even lower-paid "internships", with employers having a "take it or leave it" attitude. Most local workers, not just those in the blue collar working class, have become accustomed to working six days a week and even multiple jobs just to make ends meet; others have become rag pickers and illegal vendors, such as the elderly woman selling cakes on days when her disabled husband was feeling well enough to come along with her in his wheelchair; and some have been pushed into black-market jobs and prostitution.

Although television reports indicated the general population was very happy with receiving the one-off payment of 6,000 HKD from the government, almost everyone the researcher spoke with, from taxi driver to medical doctor, thought that the scheme was a ridiculous band-aid solution. Everyone agreed that the money should have been spent on social programs, such as those to help the elderly; they believe that the amount is neither necessary for the wealthy nor adequate for the very poor to escape from the cycle of poverty.

OCCUPY HONG KONG AND THE MAINSTREAM PRESS

According to *Occupied Times* (2012), once a symbolic movement is considered newsworthy, it begins to lose control over its story. In the US, the mainstream media coverage of the Occupy movement has included two main messages. The first message is that those involved, who are unemployed, should return home and let everyone else's lives return to normal (Chomsky 2011). The second one is that the movement does not have a political programme (*ibid*). In Hong Kong, the message was equally derisive, although the themes from the coverage at the beginning of the Occupation to the end did differ.

Most articles in the *South China Morning Post* were not blatant in their criticism. Instead, they were, as Chomsky (2012) described the American media's portrayal of the Occupy movement, dismissive; they used innocuous ways of lowering the public's perceived validity of the Occupy Central movement itself. One way of doing this was to call the movement "Occupy Central," conveying via the quotation marks the impression that they were the so-called Occupy Central. Another tactic was to discuss the movement in the context of charities which it might disturb or whose cancellation was blamed on Occupy Hong Kong, as if Occupy Central were the very anti-thesis of charity.

In these articles, the paper did not bother to criticize the global Occupy movement, but instead, it chose to invalidate the local Occupy by saying it was not really part of the international movement. Participants of the local Occupy were portrayed as mindlessly copying an international fad. It was even stated that the local Occupy was just another routine protest and redundant as Hong Kong already had activists and movements. This is as if American cities did not have progressive movements and groups before the start of Occupy. In fact, as a grassroots movement, individuals anywhere in the world who feel the local environment requires an Occupy movement are free to start one and become part of the global phenomenon.

Instead, Occupiers were portrayed as having no coherent message and just repeating meaningless slogans. As a media outlet, the *Post* failed to acknowledge to the public that all the Occupations around the world have sprouted from previous grievances; rather than acknowledging that the international Occupy movement is about social issues that many care about, the editorial line has consistently tried to separate Occupy from the social issues it tries to address, preferring to portray it as a spectacle. This frame, in fact, is used by media around the world to distance the general population from social movements (Barker 2008) and give the impression that political engagement in general is not effective (Smith 2011).

Along the same lines, the Occupiers were also frequently portrayed as just experimenting on self-governing in their commune. This plays on the us-versus-them mentality, making it difficult for the general public to relate to the Occupiers, who are cast as the "them". In fact, Occupy Central was not described as a whole grassroots organization but, rather, a disperse gathering of commune dwellers who fail to agree on a message. The hint to the public was, "Why would anyone want to support them, when they do not even support themselves?"

Around the time that the movement ended, some of the same themes were still used, while some new ones were invented. There was no acknowledgement of the fact that the Occupy movement as a whole had increased the Hong Kong public's recognition of the territory's income inequality and had made the issue a systemic, public matter, rather than an individual one. A theme that continued to be used was that the Occupy movement was not valid, just an Occupy with quotation marks, a so-called Occupy; other new themes also appeared, as discussed in the paragraphs below.

The general essence was that the Occupiers were finally being "swept" or "turfed out" (Cheung and Lee 2012), as if they had been trash to begin with. In fact, Apply Daily (2011) mentions that the protestors were often referred to as "useless youths" and told to "get a job." The members of Occupy were described as having protested at the expense of the people's convenience, when in reality, the movement was about the people to begin with. Instead of being seen as raising awareness, it was described as being a disturbance to everyone, with all its "antics"; instead of being framed as activists organizing in a meaningful way as part of an international movement, they were constructed as children playing house.

Again, to distance the reader from the movement and prevent any sympathies, the us-versus-them framework was used. In the message that "we have been tolerant towards them", the term "we" was used to refer to HSBC, the government, the general public and even the foreign domestic workers who regularly use the space under HSBC on Sundays; the term "them" referred to the Occupiers (Lo 2012).

The movement was portrayed as a failure, because even the aforementioned foreign domestic workers, those who shared the space with the Occupy camp during the period of Occupation, had no idea why the Occupiers were there at all. At least, that was what the newspaper's quote from one domestic worker suggested; the newspaper did not include any quotes from domestic workers who did understand what the Occupation was about (Choi 2012). Indeed, the author learned from the Occupiers that there were various cases in which reporters chose to use quotes from outliers on purpose to convey a negative image about the movement; there were complaints that one outlet had interviewed many Occupiers about their idea of what would help alleviate the income disparity in Hong Kong, and then this outlet proceeded to choose to only report the opinion of one particular person, whose answer was, "Love." This deliberately misleading presentation conveyed to readers that Occupy Central was a gathering of "hippies" who had little grounding in reality.

Here, it must be said that the *South China Morning Post* did not have the most negative reporting about Occupy Central. Based on first-hand accounts from the Occupiers, the researcher learned that various reporters from different outlets had appeared to be sympathetic to the cause and then turned around to write high insulting pieces. In quite an outrageous example, one seemingly friendly reporter instructed the community members to make friendly poses for the photographer, and then later, she published a highly-insulting article claiming that Occupy Hong Kong was a big orgy or party made of university students chilling out. The author located the article as one written by Hui (2011).

In the coverage examined, reporting was within the "protest paradigm", as coined by Chan and Lee (1984, as cited in Barker, 2008). One aspect of this paradigm is working to separate protesters from non-protesters (*ibid*). Another aspect is giving the impression that protests spontaneously appear and are not in the interest of the general public (Goldlust, 1980, as cited in Barker, 2008).

As a result of the negative, distorted coverage, on 15 August, 2012, Occupy Central officially declared on its Facebook page that it would no longer be doing any mainstream media interviews (Occupy Central 2012). Reliance on the Mainstream media, whether by trying to control its message or letting press response define a movement's actions, takes resources away from direct action and the use of alternative media (Davidson 2012).

LESSONS LEARNED FROM OCCUPY HONG KONG

The coming together of Occupy Hong Kong itself was a big achievement, in the researcher's opinion. Their display of an egalitarian community in the midst of Central, the financial heart of Hong Kong, was highly symbolic. In the words of Chomsky (2012), it fought the message of selfishness, countering it with that of community.

In the US, a major achievement of the movement was that it raised public recognition of income inequality to higher levels than ever (*ibid),* refocusing the debate from debts and deficit to income inequality (Waldron 2012). For the first time since the Great Depression, the issue received "front-page" attention from both the mass media and politicians (Chernus 2012). Occupy changed public conversation, which is required before policies are changed (*ibid*). No matter how Occupy Central was portrayed by the media, it succeeded in getting coverage and bringing issues of inequality more into discussion, even if it did not, according to Leung (2012), make its purpose known to the lower classes.

No movement is perfect, and there are always lessons to be learned, because the struggle towards equality requires long-term, dedicated work and learning through participation (Chomsky 2012). The fight requires activists play the "long game" since meaningful policy change can take years (Chernus 2012).

#1. Keep Strong Links with Other Community Organizations

On the first days of Occupy Hong Kong, there was much support from various civil society groups, such as those of foreign domestic workers; this showed that Occupy had succeeded in reaching out to these organizations, which felt that Occupy's message reflected their beliefs. The researcher herself joined one group of migrants as they marched from HSBC to the US Consulate and then went to join the official Occupy event in Exchange Square. Another group that showed support included the Anti-Lehman Brothers protesters, comprised of investors who had lost their savings due to the institution's scandalous bankruptcy. Various progressive political figures, such as Leung Kwok Hung, who is popularly known as Longhair and from the League of Social Democrats, and Sally Tang from Socialist Action, who set up booths and/or came to show physical support for the movement. However, after the initial period, support quickly tapered off as the Occupiers were regarded as being closed to cooperation, such as via jointly called actions.

Although the Occupiers did show up at some civil society events, even when they joined under the banner of Occupy, it was perceived by groups that they were no longer reaching out and were not receptive to opportunities to cooperate. Numerous political and NGO groups, such as those working with migrants, had tried to approach them, but these groups communicated to the author that they had felt shunned.

The lesson here would be that other groups with common goals are allies and their members are potential supporters. It is necessary to keep dialogue and cooperation open with these community groups. While there is a need to accentuate the class division between the 1% and the 99% (Dean 2011), there is also a need for the 99% to stand together in solidarity. In order for progressives to be ready to challenge the system, their communities must be closely linked (CrimethInc. Workers'

Collective, n.d.a). When participants and witnesses personally experience mass action, news about the action and its message is spread through word of mouth, social media and other noncorporate communication channels (*ibid*); this not only makes it difficult for the mainstream media to ignore the action without losing credibility (*ibid*), more importantly, it allows movements to reach out directly to the general public.

#2. HAVE REALISTIC EXPECTATIONS TOWARDS THE MAINSTREAM PRESS

For those seeking social change, the media is a line of the fight (Occupied Times 2012). The media is known to shape public opinion in a way that protects market interests and the status quo (Davidson 2012; Occupied Times 2012). Although it is understandable that Occupy Central was annoyed with the press for negative and distorted portrayals, this type of coverage is to be expected from the mainstream media, and there is nothing to be gained from either antagonizing the media by officially cutting them off or playing to them. The suggestion is to ignore the spin and not let it define activists' actions (Davidson 2012; Occupied Times 2012). Instead, movements need focus campaigns less on the mainstream media, and more on their own creativity and proactivity in reaching the public (Davidson 2012).

Instead of being defined by the media, the movement needs to creatively use it as a tool for subversive empowerment, to raise awareness and liberate the mind (*ibid*). For example, knowing the nature of the mainstream media, it is important to act swiftly, go undetected and catch them off guard so that they broadcast events without being prepared (CrimethInc. Workers' Collective, n.d.a). At the same time, it is also necessary to understand that, given the mainstream media's interest in preserving the status quo, subsequent actions will not receive as much coverage since the media will be prepared (*ibid*).

Instead of relying on the mainstream media to speak out, activists need to find alternative ways to speak to people directly and counterbalance the mainstream construction of a movement (Occupied Times 2012). While some say there is a need for activists need to work together to improve the mainstream media, which they seem forced to work within (Barker 2008), others argue that—instead of trying to beat the mainstream media at their game—there is a need to expand underground or alternative channels (CrimethInc. Workers' Collective, n.d.b).

It is clear that what movements need are not just "product placements" within the mainstream media but direct action (Occupied Times 2012). Activists need to use direct action activities outside of the main political channels, such as radical visual events (Schossboeck 2012) and community-based actions, engaging the street through popular theatre and other, less mediated, formats. A sketch of further ideas for direct action follows.

#3. REACH OUT TO THE PUBLIC

Although internal discussion is important in a community of freedom (Chomsky 2012), there seemed to be too much focus on these internal debates at the beginning, when the movement had more support and could have used that momentum to gain even wider, further support from the public. According to Leung (2012), the public became quite indifferent to Occupy Hong Kong, and he attributes this to the failure of the local movement to reach out to the general public and come to a common understanding with them. To motivate people to act for themselves, they must be contacted more directly and touched personally (CrimethInc. Workers' Collective, n.d.b).

According to Chomsky (2012), there is a need for activists to go out and join the public wherever they are, getting involved in their activities and reaching out to the general community. There is a need for movements to not only hold protests, but also to carry out direct action, such as growing food and providing free child care (CrimethInc. Workers' Collective (n.d.a). This is what many, both individuals and NGOs, proposed that Occupy Central do from the beginning. Several Occupiers conveyed to the author their wish to start a separate Occupy camp within Hong Kong in order to do so, but they either did not receive enough support or had to attend to other responsibilities taking them away from the territory. For example, foreign domestic worker groups had suggested linking Occupy with the surrounding foreign domestic worker community, which regularly spent Sundays in the financial district, but this never happened. Although nearing the end of the Occupation, there appeared a new member who located edible food items which had been discarded by supermarkets, and then handed this food out to the homeless in Hong Kong and invited the homeless to stay at the camp; but by that time, it was too late.

Due to inaction in this area, the general public did not feel like the movement touched their lives in any way; unless they happened to go to the financial district—which many people in Hong Kong generally do not do—and walk by the Occupy camp, the mainstream media provided most of the information they knew about Occupy.

CONCLUSION

The situation of poverty on the ground, which serves as both the background and the very reason for Occupy Hong Kong, is dire and heart-breaking. The situation of most could be termed wage slavery. For a place that claims to be a world-class city, Hong Kong's *laissez-faire* attitude towards the vulnerable is nauseating.

In a city with astronomically expensive rent and low wages, the regular people have been reduced to living a subsistence existence. While many slave away as janitors or rag pickers just to live in cage/coffin homes, they can look around nearby to see the luxury in which those who have benefited from their exploitation live; the expensive condominiums and shopping centres have cropped up everywhere, thanks to government preferences favouring the development of luxury buildings over public housing which has a many years-long waiting list, and these more spacious condos are not for the regular folk. Often, they are actually cheaper per square foot. In the past, people might have looked to these buildings and hoped to one day live and shop in them, but there is no longer the sense of hope as the gap between rich and poor is only getting wider. Old people who did whatever they had to in order to guarantee their children an education and improve their future have discovered that there are not enough living-wage jobs to go around; while they live in horrible conditions, some say all they look forward to is dying.

It is in this context that, as part of the global Occupy movement, Occupy Hong Kong came along as a movement that tried to help to change things. The *South China Morning Post's* reportage was within what Chan and Lee coined as the "protest paradigm" (1984, as cited in Barker, 2008). Instead of being portrayed as members of the working poor, which many of the participants were, they were framed as *petit bourgeois*, university students or children with little better to do than to play house, pretend be part of an international movement and disturb the rest of the population, including the poor they were trying to represent. The Occupiers had been framed as the "them", and somehow, all the poor and oppressed people had become "us" with the privileged and powerful.

In the face of such income disparity and financial oppression, the development of Occupy Central was especially commendable. However, as with all movements, there are lessons to be learned for next time.

There is a need to keep strong links with other community organizations and stand together with other progressive people as part of the 99% fighting the 1%; Occupy Central became increasing isolated as it was perceived by other groups that they were no longer as open and receptive to cooperation. Standing together not only builds critical mass but also allows a movement and its message to spread through word of mouth, social media and other channels outside of mainstream media, forcing the mainstream to cover the issue.

At the same time, movements must have realist expectations towards the mainstream press, who act as protectors of market interests and the status quo. Instead of fighting for "product placement" in the press, being disappointed with mainstream narratives and then officially cutting off contact with the press, it is best to understand that this is the way the mainstream media operates and ignore their reportage instead of letting it define future actions. Other alternatives include using the media creatively, expanding alternative media channels to communicate to the public and using direct action. Using methods such as street theatre, radical visual events and pirate radio stations, movements can bypass the mainstream media and raise awareness more directly and spark critical thinking.

Movements must also reach out and touch the broader general public with direct messages rather than focusing too heavily on the specifics of internal debates. Many NGOs and individuals, both within and without the local encampment, had suggested this, but these recommendations were ignored. Due to inaction in this area, the general public received most of their information from the mainstream media and did not feel the movement had touched their lives. Examples of possible alternatives mentioned above include community-based actions, whether these be in neighborhoods or workplaces which address immediate needs, such as by growing food, providing childcare and reaching out to the homeless and isolated. These actions not only allow for movements to circumnavigate the Mainstream media but also allow for meaningful dialogue breaking down the artificial separation between the general public and members of the movement.

With Hong Kong's disgraceful situation of income disparity and injustice, it needed a local Occupy movement, and it was admirable that people were brave enough to lead the way and start one there. The struggle for more equality does not end when authorities have removed one's camp, and this struggle must continue in Hong Kong in various forms, taking into account the lessons learned from this experience. Indeed, with plans for Occupy Central II in 2014, this time in the form of a road blockade to fight for universal suffrage in the territory, the movement continues to be the centre of public discussion in Hong Kong (But and Cheung 2013). Around the world, there need to be more and more of the 99% that stand together to demand change from governments, both via global movements, such as Occupy, and local, community-based actions centred around neighborhoods and workplaces, for example. There needs to be recognition that the world is increasingly being divided into two classes, the elite and precariat, and the precariat need to work collectively instead of competing to climb the social ladder, harbouring unrealistic dreams of becoming one of the elite. The fight for the oppressed must go on, as it is a long, continuous project, while each should remember that people with power don't give this power up unless they have to (Chomsky 2012).

REFERENCES

Barker, M. 2008. "Mass Media and Social Movements: A Critical Examination of the Relation between the Mainstream Media and Social Movements." *Global Research*. http://www.globalresearch.ca/mass-media-and-social-movements/8761 (04 Feb 2013).

But, J. and Cheung, G. 2013. "Occupy Central Pioneer Outlines its Four-stage Plan to Achieve Democracy." *South China Morning Post*, April 2. http://www.scmp.com/news/hong-kong/article/1201313/occupy-central-pioneer-outlines-its-four-stage-plan-achieve-democracy (02 Apr 2013).

Butler, J. 2011. "For and Against Precarity." In *Tidal: Occupy Theory, Occupy Strategy 1* (December 2011): 12-13. https://docs.google.com/file/d/0B8k8g5Bb3BxdcHI0bXZTbVpUbGVQSnRLSG4zTEx1QQ/edit (4 Feb 2013).

Census and Statistics Department. 2012. "2011 Report on Annual Earning and Hours Survey." Census and Statistics Department, Hong Kong. http://www.statistics.gov.hk/pub/B10500142011AN11B0100.pdf (07 Dec 2012).

Chen, T.-P. 2012. "Hong Kong's Wealth Gap Gets Larger." *The Wall Street Journal (*19 June) http://blogs.wsj.com/chinarealtime/2012/06/19/hong-kongs-wealth-gap-gets-larger/ (07 Dec 2012).

Chernus, I. 2012. "Occupy Obama on Election Day." *Common Dreams*, 5 (November) https://www.commondreams.org/view/2012/11/05-1 (11 May 2013).

Cheung, S. and Lee, A. 2012. "Armed with Court Order, Bailiffs Sweep Occupy Activists from HSBC Site." *South China Morning Post* (12 September) http://www.scmp.com/news/hong-kong/article/1034493/armed-court-order-bailiffs-sweep-occupy-activists-hsbc-site (07 Dec 2012).

Choi, C. 2012. "Few Activists Left on Eve of Occupy Central Closure." *South China Morning Post* (27 August) http://www.scmp.com/news/hong-kong/article/1022991/few-activists-left-eve-occupy-central-closure (07 Dec 2012).

Chomsky, N. 2012. *Occupy*. London: Penguin Books.

Chui, L., Leung, S.T. and Yip, C.H. 2012. "Income Inequality in Hong Kong." Ho Lap College. http://www.hkss.org.hk/SPC/2011-12/AwardPDF/S11-12-DP4.pdf (08 Dec 2012).

CIA 2013. *The World Factbook*. Washington D.C.: Central Intelligence Agency. https://www.cia.gov/library/publications/the-world-factbook/geos/mc.html (22 Jan 2013).

CrimethInc. Workers' Collective (n.d.a) "Demonstrating Resistance: Mass Action and Autonomous Action in the Election Year." CrimethInc. Workers' Collective. http://www.crimethinc.com/texts/atoz/demonstrating.php (05 Feb 2013).

CrimethInc. Workers' Collective (n.d.b). "Working 'Within the System': If
    you beat them at their own game, you've lost." CrimethInc. Workers'
    Collective. http://www.crimethinc.com/texts/atoz/demonstrating.php (05
    Feb 2013).

Davidson, K. 2012. "Media as Direct Action." *Tidal: Occupy Theory,
    Occupy Strategy 2:* 26-27.
    https://docs.google.com/file/d/0B8k8g5Bb3BxdNXB3dkgweEhUTnFiTn
    VOTVFyZUJxQQ/edit (04 Feb 2013).

Dean, J. 2011. "Claiming Division, Naming a Wrong." *Theory & Event*: 14
    (4), 2011 Supplement. http://muse.jhu.edu/login?
    auth=0&type=summary&url=/journals/theory_and_event/v014/14.4S.dea
    n01.html (05 Feb 2013).

Demographia. 2012. *8th Annual Demographia International Housing
    Affordability Survey.* http://www.demographia.com/dhi.pdf (07 Dec
    2012).

DeWolf, C. 2010. "FM 101: Hong Kong's pirate radio station survives."
    *CNN Travel (*05 August) http://travel.cnn.com/hong-kong/radio-stations-
    hong-kong-907769 (03 Feb 2013)

Drysdale, P. 2012. "Can Asia help power world recovery?" *East Asia Forum*,
    (18 June) http://www.eastasiaforum.org/2012/06/18/can-asia-help-power-
    world-recovery/ (03 Feb 2013).

Einhorn, B. 2009. "Countries with the Biggest Gaps Between Rich and
    Poor." *BusinessWeek*, (13 October) http://images.businessweek.com/ss/
    09/10/1013_biggest_rich_poor_gap_globally/1.htm (22 Feb 2011)

Fisher, S. 2012. "Poverty commission must make most vulnerable their
    priority." *South China Morning Post*, (24 October)
    http://www.scmp.com/comment/insight-opinion/article/1068061/poverty-
    commission-must-make-most-vulnerable-their-priority (10 Dec 2012).

Goodman, A. and Moynihan, D. 2012. *The Silenced Majority: Stories of
    Uprisings, Occupations, Resistance, and Hope.* Chicago: Haymarket
    Books.

Henrard, V. 2012. "Income Inequality and Public Expenditure on Social
    Policy in Hong Kong." *Civic Exchange.* http://www.civic-
    exchange.org/wp/wp-content/uploads/2011/07/110729
    IncomeInequality.pdf (08 Dec 2012).

Hui, Z. Y. 2011. U 仔烏托邦　佔領滙豐變 hea 竇. *Face*, (11 November).
    http://hk.face.nextmedia.com/template/face/art_main.php?
    iss_id=236&sec_id=14988689&art_id=15842562 (10 Dec 2012).

InMediaHK. 2011. "Hong Kong: Occupy Central." *Hong Kong:
    InMediaHK.* [Video] http://acopy.net/en/content/hong-kong-occupy-
    central (03 Feb 2013).

Lam, C.L. 2011. 我們真正需要佔領什麼 ?*Left21*. (15 October)
    http://left21.hk/wp/2011/10/%E6%88%91%E5%80%91%E7%9C%9F
    %E6%AD%A3%E9%9C%80%E8%A6%81%E4%BD

%94%E9%A0%98%E4%BB%80%E9%BA%BC%EF%BC%9F/ (03 Feb 2013).

Lau, K.Y. 2012. 實拍香港「棺材房」1.4 平米月租 1450 港幣(圖). *Ta Kung Pao*, (16 October) http://www.takungpao.com.hk/house/content/2012-10/16/content_1237495_2.htm (04 Feb 2013).

Leung, K. 2012. 通識攻略：佔領中環成與敗. *The Sun*, (12 September) http://the-sun.on.cc/cnt/news/20120912/00661_001.html (10 Dec 2012).

Occupied Times. 2012. "Editorial: October 2012." *Occupied Times*, (15 October) http://theoccupiedtimes.co.uk/?p=7297 (05 Feb 2013).

Lo, A. 2012. "Occupy Central, It's Time to Pack up." *South China Morning Post*, (31 August) http://www.scmp.com/comment/insight-opinion/article/1026565/occupy-central-its-time-pack (07 Dec 2012).

Occupy Central. 2012. "Occupy Central Will Not Be Doing Anymore Mainstream Media Interviews." *Occupy Central.* https://www.facebook.com/notes/occupy-central-%E4%BD%94%E9%A0%98%E4%B8%AD%E7%92%B0/occupy-central-will-not-be-doing-anymore-mainstream-media-interviews/351463661600145 (07 Dec 2012).

Ropp, R.S. 2010. *China in World History*. Oxford: Oxford University Press.

Scheme6000. 2011. "Scheme $6000 計劃." *Scheme6000* http://www.scheme6000.gov.hk/eng/index.html (07 Dec 2012).

Schossboeck, J. 2012. "The Great Debate: Can Occupy Achieve Its Political Goals by Remaining Outside of Main-stream Politics? Against." *Occuped Times*, (11 February) http://theoccupiedtimes.co.uk/?p=2377 (05 Feb 2014).

Smith, J. 2011). "How Elite Media Strategies Marginalize the Occupy Movement." *CommonDreams.org*, (11 December). http://www.commondreams.org/view/2011/12/11-5 (04 Feb 2013).

Society for Community Organisation. 2012. "Sojourning as tempura - Inadequate Housing Photo Exhibition." *Society for Community Organisation* http://www.soco.org.hk/artwalk2012/index.htm (04 Feb 2013).

Varon, J. 2012. "They Are Not Afraid." *Journal for Occupied Studies*. http://occupiedstudies.org/articles/they-are-not-afraid.html (04 Feb 2013).

Waldron, T. 2012. "After Six Months, A Look at What Occupy Wall Street Has Accomplished." *ThinkProgress* (19 March) http://thinkprogress.org/economy/2012/03/19/447087/after-six-months-a-look-at-what-occupy-wall-street-has-accomplished/ (11 May 2013).

[arts & culture]

'Art Through a Birch Bark Heart': An Illustrated Interview with Erin Marie Konsmo

*WITH **PJ LILLEY**[1]*

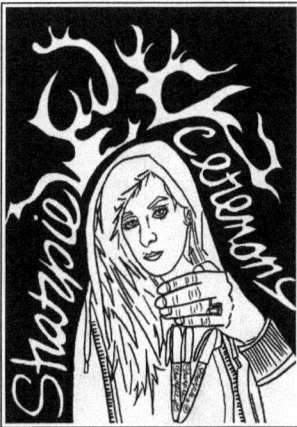

Erin Marie Konsmo is the Media Arts and Projects Coordinator for the Native Youth Sexual Health Network. She is Métis/Cree from the historic Métis communities of Onoway/Lac St. Anne, Alberta. She is a self-taught community-engaged visual and multi-media Indigenous artist, supporting community to create their own art and expressions around sexual and reproductive health, rights and justice. Her art practice is based in community spaces, culture, and Indigenous led media and arts initiatives.

Erin is currently serving as one of the North American focal points for the Global Indigenous Youth Caucus at the United Nations Permanent Forum on Indigenous Issues. She holds a Bachelor of Arts in Sociology from the University of Calgary and a Master of Environmental Studies from York University,

---

[1] Besides this interview, PJ is the production editor for this journal. She can be reached via <pj@radicalcriminology.org>

with a concentration in environmental and reproductive health. (See more at http://erinkonsmo.blogspot.ca)

For *Radical Criminology*, PJ spoke with Erin in July 2013...

PJ Lilley: It's nice to "meet" you. Thank you for taking the time with us, as it seems to me that the themes in your work overlap and carry through many similarities with the themes of our journal. Your work conveys strong images, life and death, the impacts of extractive industries, such as the tar sands' environmental destruction heavy upon women's bodies, contrasted the with the fierce beauty and strength of women in resistance, the struggle for life lived with full self-determination.

"Discovery Is Toxic : Indigenous Women on the Frontline of Environmental and Reproductive Justice". April 2012.

I noticed also several pieces of your artwork seem useful as 'agit-prop', and much of your blog portfolio seems to be work that you've done as posters for various organizations, conferences, public events or actions. Could you begin by talking a bit about the process of your art practice?

Erin Marie Konsmo: I'll start with where the art has come from in my life. I go back to who has brought the creative tendencies into my life. Art has always been an important part of who I am and how I grew up. I've had strong mentors in art throughout, the two strongest ones were my mom and my grandmother. Art was a really important way for me to express myself growing up, even as a young child. Like my mom (and grandma) always said, "keep your hands busy." Arts and crafts were one way to do that, we kept our hands busy. I remember pressing flowers with my grandmother, seeing her carve wood, and using materials like birch-bark. My mom is also a truly creative person as well. It might not be a formal artistic practice, but it was about the practice of being creative and doing something with our hands. As an Indigenous youth, I found that there was no way to express the feelings of going through a decolonization process, of reconnecting with culture, and understanding all of the things that I was seeing and feeling without going back to that art practice. Going back to art was out of necessity; it wasn't this luxury, it was something that I felt I *had* to go back to, and so that was the beginning, of how I came back to it—this process of having no other way, except through that, to work through those feelings. So began that larger practice of connecting back to community and back to self—and there being a lot of difficult things to go through with that process. Once it really started, it did connect to my work with community, so I often describe myself as a "self-taught artist" in that I don't have any actual formal artistic training, so I say I'm a self-taught, community-engaged, visual multimedia Indigenous artist.

I work with multiple mediums, and that's almost out of necessity as well. As an Indigenous person, I've found I've needed multiple mediums in order to convey the layers of expression around any given subject. We have to find multiple different ways to express our voice. I really started back in with the visual arts, but since then, it's moved into needing to incorporate video and sound. I've started to pull in more traditional materials. Birchbark, for example, is very important to me. This traditional material has become an expression of my identity, of where I come from. I've named my blog "Artwork from a Birchbark Heart"; birchbark has been something that has been really "hands-on" for me, and it has helped me to work through a personal healing process. The layers of birch bark have a spiritual connection that I see connected to my body.

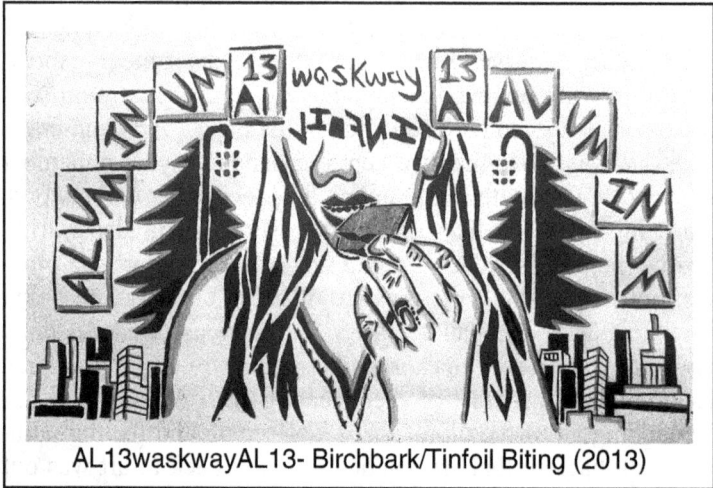

AL13waskwayAL13- Birchbark/Tinfoil Biting (2013)

A lot of my artwork has been done for specific actions, events, or responding to issues. There's so much talent around us, so many talented, intelligent, expressive Indigenous youth around us, but there's also really huge obstacles to being able to express Indigenous worldviews in a way that's going to make people actually want to stop and listen to what we have to say. Whenever I've been asked to create by community, it's felt like, "if I have that gift"—and I've been told by elders, by people around me—if I have that gift of art, it's important for me to share.

PJ: Art in the service of the movement...?

EMK: Yes, art isn't just something for me to have. In fact, I often feel uncomfortable if I'm just doing art for myself. It doesn't make sense to me as a process.

PJ: Yes, it conveys the sense that the process is very much related to the finished product. I noticed there are often layers of 'text' in your images, written messages, even slogans.

EMK: Yes, people often refer to it as "your art" or they use these kind of very individualistic possessive pronouns to describe it, but I react to that, because I feel like it's community-owned. The messages and themes that come out of them are built around joint experiences, community experiences of working through things, like an expression of ceremony in response to missing and murdered Indigenous women, or around environmental violence from major extractive industries. Those understandings have been built through the work that I do on a day-to-day basis with the NYSHN, with grassroots organizations that are led by Indigenous peoples, groups like Families of Sisters in Spirit,[2] and by Indigenous youth, by conversations with my friends. It's a collective process and a collective resistance through art.

PJ: The art does seem like it's a conversation in process. Do you tend to work alone, or often as a group production? When you're working on a poster for a group action, how does that happen, as a back and forth, or is it more of a solitary process?

EMK: Like any other kind of product or outcome or action that's meant for community, the process looks different for every piece, but generally, a lot of it involves having a conversation with people. We talk about it, "this is something we would like to express through art"... Sometimes there are direct needs, people say "we need this for this action" or "it's for a presentation", or "we want to move the agenda forward and we want art to be central", to present the ideas or issues that we want to put forward.

I've also been really careful about what I share publicly. I try to be aware of what knowledge I share through my art, how it is portrayed and how it will be received. In some of my pieces, I've been really careful to ask the community, or follow up with the elders, and ask, "is this ok for me to share in my art?" Protocol is a part of my artistic practice.

There are also pieces that have been more individual to my lived experiences. The environmental justice and reproductive justice pieces of my work, of which there are many—that has

---

[2] See their group profile, on page 97

come from the place where I grew up, and seeing those connections was definitely something that I grew up with. Once I started doing more work with the NYSHN, and working with Indigenous women internationally, that's when I was able to express more of what I saw growing up. But, again, it's often when I've been in those community spaces that those expressions, visually, have been creatively supported. It's been really important to not just have those reflections of myself, but to have them engage at national levels, at international levels, for other people to reflect those same things back. That's where I have that moment, where I have that sense of empowerment, that there are people around me, that we're facing the same thing, that we're reflecting on the same issues. I feel that I was able to express that in an image.

An artist isn't supposed to say this, but I have a really hard time making art. Part of that comes back to that point in my life where I stopped altogether, because of traumatic events and losing family members. My art work also conveys and is built out of very real issues about missing and murdered Indigenous women, about consent, etc. Something that I've become more and more interested in is some of the violence that can come out of art practice.   It's not something I've fully worked through yet, but I'm engaging with more Indigenous people and Indigenous artists who do this kind of social commentary in their work.

PJ: You mean the violence brought up when remembering, when going through a healing process? How do you mean the "violence comes out of the art"?

EMK: Yes, well, part of it is it being a really heavy process to work through this art. There definitely is a lot of ceremony behind it. There's a certain level of understanding behind it, when artists are able to put down visually, or through sound, that which opens up a path to your heart, that is really visible, vulnerable.

PJ: Immersion in toxics threats/risk is something you're raising in several of the pieces, though, in your "Sharpie Ceremony", where you're smudging with sharpie fumes, and it struck me as intense in a chosen way. But, it seems like a lot of your work hits right at the gut, it has a 'low-blow' so to speak. For example the prison bars right in the pregnant womb, or the woman pole dancing. We look to publish more writings in our future issues around the decriminalization of sex work and also reproductive self-determination, which seems to be a major recurring theme in your work, so I hope we can have further collaboration with some of these pieces in the future.

EMK: Yes, some of them are really controversial. I've done the social commentary in my art for a longer period of time now and I've started to see more people's reactions and the effects of the art and what pieces are taken up over others, and why people choose to use them. So it's more of a reflective practice.

Also, I don't actually own a lot of my artwork, or I don't have it anymore; a lot of my pieces are actually made to be gifted. Gifting is a regular practice in Indigenous communities. A lot of the pieces you see on the blog are in people's homes or have traveled to different communities to be gifted.

PJ: And you've shown publicly at an exhibit here in Vancouver, too, last year at Rhizome?

EMK: Yeah, I've done a couple of different exhibits. It's not something that I've made a priority, but maybe it will happen more in the future, more showings. I continue to strive for my work to be shared in community based space. People keep telling me to show my art more in exhibits, but the majority of my showing just happens in the community, they're used as teaching tools, or in different ways of engagement.

PJ: Such visualizations must be helpful for youth in learning processes. So this has application in the kind of workshops that you do around sexual health for young people?

EMK: Yes, we work around a full spectrum of sexual and reproductive health rights and justice. There's a number of themes in the artwork that we work around at the Native Youth Sexual Health Network and a huge one has been connecting environmental violence to issues of sexual and reproductive health in the last couple of years. These pieces have been created and help us as a community to talk about those connections... whether that's increased rates of sexual violence, or increased drug and alcohol use—with no simultaneous increase in harm reduction services in communities—when resource extraction industries come in. Thus, there's messages around consent and violence in my work, also around HIV, midwifery, many related themes in our workshops.

PJ: I really enjoyed the works on midwifery, and had noticed it as a continuing theme. (It reminded me of something else I wanted to share with you around the colonial repression of midwives throughout history, and a comparison of the suppression of witchcraft with that of midwifery.[3]) It was an idea that I saw running through your various works, which was the concept of healing through birth, pregnancies both literal and figurative in process, the pains of art works being "born".

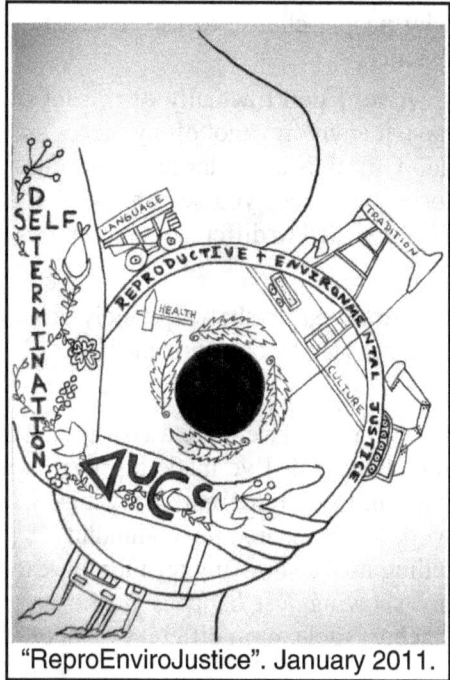

"ReproEnviroJustice". January 2011.

---

[3] Ehrenreich, Barbara and Deirdre English. 1973. *Witches, Midwives, and Nurses: A History of Women Healers*. New York: The Feminist Press, CUNY. http://tmh.floonet.net/articles/witches.html

EMK: Yes, my coworker has talked about the process of my art creation relating to birth. We were trying to talk about how my art practice had developed over the last couple years and I was trying to express my frustration around, well, there's very much this Western sense of what making art is, what that practice is and how it didn't seem to fit at all with what I do. There is an Indigenous process of protocol and creation for my art. That was one way that made sense for the work that we're already doing around sexual and reproductive health. You know, that it takes a community to pull together and do that birthing process, just like it takes communities to make these images. They're community driven, community born. These art pieces will have whole life cycles. They start from their birth in conversations, the triggering event, sometimes traumatic events, sometimes out of absolute necessity, say for increasing the profile of an issue. They come back at different points and mature with age and have different meanings taken up within them. Some of them were created four or five years ago, but they are picked up again when there's new layers added to the issue. People will say "now I see there's this in the artwork."

My borders piece just got picked up quite a bit more in the past month, because it was shared by No One Is Illegal and Idle No More for use in movements around border issues....

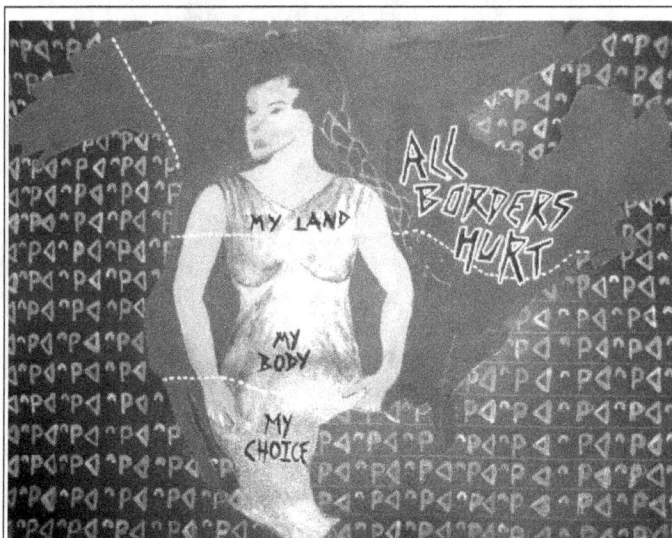

"No Borders". March 2011.

So they have these life cycles, these artworks, like a person has life cycles as well. And that's an appreciation I have, that art just doesn't have these static moments, they're meant to, and do have, whole life cycles. And sometimes they disappear too, or they become irrelevant to the conversation so they die off.

PJ: I noticed throughout your work that you refer to the large numbers of Indigenous women inside the prison industrial complex... and that a lot of your focus was towards the Canadian state. (Perhaps as you travel through the American state, you find similar themes; I'm not as clear on what the percentage of Indigenous women is within the US prison system—though there is some research comparing holdings of people of color in the public & private systems in the US published in this issue[4] and the next of this journal—but clearly it's overwhelmingly disproportionate.) So I'm wondering, in terms of your art practice, how you take that conflict with the state in "agitational propaganda" so to speak. You mention use by No One is Illegal, for example, take even something so simple as saying "NO BORDERS", it's a pretty big assertion. So I guess my question is, how do you see your art helping us to get from where we are now at this moment, to where we want to be?

EMK: Well, first of all, I've never had anybody refer to my art as "agitational propaganda"! *laughs*

PJ: Yes, I guess I use that word 'agit-prop' a lot... I noticed it in regards to thinking of your art in terms

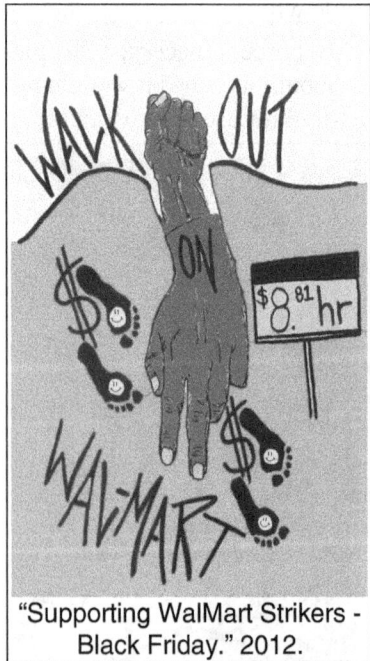

"Supporting WalMart Strikers - Black Friday." 2012.

---

[4]For these statistics, see page 139 of this journal, on *The Color of Prisons*, by Christopher Petrella & Josh Begley.

of how it could be layed out in a design for use as street art/ ie. you've left space for a meeting point... and in several you've used large striking images with a lot of whitespace. So I thought it seemed like it was designed to be useful for street application... and this is related to the question of your political practice...

EMK: Sure. Talking about the prisons, and the high rate of Indigenous women in the prison industrial complex (PIC) and the larger issue of the PIC coming out into these issues of policing in our lives, whether that's around our bodies, whether that's around medical health services, it's been something that... once again ... we have to talk about because it's always there. We can't **not** talk about the PIC because it extends into all reaches of our lives as Indigenous peoples, as Indigenous youth, and women in particular. One particular experience I remember is: I was at Aamjiwnaang [Chippewas of Sarnia] First Nation and members of the local community were taking me around and showing me Chemical Valley[5]... and we were talking about Alberta [Tar Sands]. In both struggles, youth are putting themselves, their bodies on the line, to defend their families, literally from dying.

So we were in a restaurant in Sarnia, and here on the wall, there was a frame with a police badge in it. The badge had industry depicted inside of it, and it was the actual symbol of the police in Sarnia, and I was, like, OMG, that is the most honest representation! It breaks down exactly as the "prison" "industry"...there's the industry, the pumps, and there's the state, the badge, there it all is, open and obvious. That's where, just last month, Ron Plain was given a $16,000 fine for holding up the railway.[6]

---

[5] See sidebar (following page) "At Aamjiwnaang in Chemical Valley", an excerpt from *Environmental Health Perspectives,* Dec. 2012

[6] For more information on his prosecution for the Aamijiwnaang community's stand during the 'Idle No More' December 2012 CN Rail blockade, read his blog at http://ronplain.wordpress.com/2013/06/17/a-derailed-christmas-my-story/

AT AAMJIWNAANG IN CHEMICAL VALLEY

"The reserve is surrounded by 62 major industrial facilities located within 25 km, including oil refineries, chemical manufacturers (40% of Canada's chemical industry), and manufacturers of plastics, polymers, and agricultural products. The area is known as "Chemical Valley." Levels of air pollutants, including volatile organic compounds, are high. In 1996, hospital admissions for women in Chemical Valley were 3.11 times the expected rates for women and 2.83 times those for men than would be expected based on other rates for Ontario. These admissions were especially pronounced for cardiovascular and respiratory ailments, and were hypothesized to be pollution related. About 40% of Aamjiwnaang residents require use of an inhaler, and 17% of adults and 22% of children are reported to have asthma. The ratio of male births declined over the period 1984–1992 from > 0.5 to about 0.3, a change that may at least partly reflect effects of chemical exposures. Releases of chemicals have also interfered with the community's cultural life, affecting hunting, fishing, medicine gathering, and ceremonial activities." ---

Excerpt by: Hoover, Elizabeth & Katsi Cook, Ron Plain, Kathy Sanchez, Vi Waghiyi, Pamela Miller, Renee Dufault, Caitlin Sislin, and David O. Carpenter *from* "Indigenous Peoples of North America: Environmental Exposures and Reproductive Justice" in *Environmental Health Perspectives*. 2012 December; 120(12): 1645–1649. http://dx.doi.org/10.1289/ehp.1205422

Yet this is going to happen more and more... that self-determination, and standing up for the rights of our communities is
going to end up with more and more Indigenous youth, Indigenous women and communities in jail. They're set up for Indigenous communities by this point! They're set up so that in
the event that we stand up for the defense of self-determination,
the rights of our communities, the state can try to contain the
dissent. Yet, Indigenous peoples have been doing this for a
long period of time, and I recognize that—just because I'm a
young person, and I'm really angry—I recognize that there are
people that have been doing this for years. But there is a really
stark thing that is happening right now, with so many people
standing up, so many Indigenous youth standing up, well, the
prisons are just going to start to be filled up with us. It really is
across the board in North America; there are really stark rates
of Indigenous women and youth in US prisons as well as Canadian prisons. We see mandatory minimum drug sentences that
have been put into place in Canada, which is clearly modeled
after the US system. So, anyone who says "oh the US is way
worse than Canada" isn't really seeing the realities of the prison
system in Canada, where it's a really bad situation.

"Industry Off My Ovaries".
September 2011.

PJ: And have you done work within Indigenous forms of justice, held healing circles, been part of restorative justice programs?

EMK: Yes, I would say that's in our day-to-day work, expressing what we understand to be Indigenous forms of justice, even in the way that we build ourselves as Indigenous people.   I do see youth taking care of each other when things happen.   I see them making active choices around whether or not they involve police, whether or not they involve Child Welfare, and that can be as simple as them instead asking an elder to come in and deal with a conflict.   I've had to do that with the stuff that's happened in my life; it's making that active choice to talk to an elder or a community leader instead, and say, "can you come in and help with this issue?"

PJ: So it is a matter of creating the alternatives as we go...?

EMK: Yes, and it's messy.

PJ: Well, it's good if you can continue to reflect that in your artwork, to write and speak about it, because I think there are a lot of people struggling to find justice—native and non-native. Especially on the streets, or under-housed, in crowded situations of housing.   Here in Surrey, and Vancouver, where rent is so incredibly high, you see a lot more situations of domestic abuse, where people (most often women) are putting up with awful situations because of the housing crisis. So talking about ways where there can be an intervention, even at the community level, even a large scale intervention, without bringing in the state. ... Well, I just think that your experiences with that type of thing are a very valuable thing to try to communicate. If I can encourage you to try to continue with that, I do think a lot of people are looking for that.

EMK: So these should be my next five art pieces! *laughs*

But more about my art in terms of detaching from dependence on the state: I think sometimes sexual and reproductive health and justice isn't looked at as a serious way of decolonization, of building up Indigenous nationhood. But I do think people can learn more about self-determination, about sovereignty, about what nationhood means, about breaking down these borders and barriers and removal of dependancy on the state from looking at what's been learned by the reproductive justice movement. That's been one aspect of my artwork—the importance of the reproductive justice movement within anti-colonial movements in general—that needs to be taken more seriously.

PJ: I was going to foreground that—the colonial imposition of the Indian Act and how the lineage was purposefully cut off by the state, how if you married out or left the reserve, they could try to cut off "status"—by reading a section from the chapter of the book *Speaking My Truth* on the "Legacy of Residential Schools: Missing and Murdered Aboriginal Women" by Beverley Jacobs and Andrea Williams:

> While initially inclusive of men and women, along with their marriage partners and children, the legislation was quickly amended to exclude non-Indian men who married Indian women but not non-Indian women who married Indian men. The Report of the Royal Commission on Aboriginal Peoples (RCAP) noted: "For the first time, Indian status began to be associated with the male line of descent." The 1857 Gradual Civilization Act furthered the distinction between the standing of men and women by providing a route for Indian men, but not women, to renounce their status "in order to join non-Aboriginal colonial society." The legal means, referred to as 'enfranchisement,' to voluntarily give up Indian status was granted only to men who met a specific set of criteria: for example, over the age of 21; able to read and write English or French; educated; free of debt; and 'of good moral character'. The wives and children of enfranchised men automatically lost their status.

It spoke further about the Victorian imposition of who was "of good moral character". The Indian Agents reserved the right to continue to determine whether or not women were included in that category; sometimes if they weren't married, or if there was a child born out of marriage, they would be excluded —even if their Nation decided to *include* them—the Indian Agent could come in and formally exclude them and so many people lost status that way. Clearly it was a way of breaking the sense that, as John Trudell put it, "we're all human beings"—in being all human—so that Original Peoples were continually interfered with, attempted to be broken up by the

Indian Act processes of colonization. Also the matter of forced sterilizations contributed to this process, officially only ending in the 70's.

In Alberta, the 'Sterilization Act' of 1928 (started under the father of right-wing politician Preston Manning) specifically targeted people in mental health institutions, but also aimed at native women, new immigrants, the disabled, unwed mothers, women accused of lesbian 'tendencies', and so on. It was only finally ended in 1972, after sterilizing more than 2,000 Albertans. [7]

Have you come across women that are grappling with these issues?

EMK: Yep, that was one of the most annoying aspects of the feminist movement's constant refrain about "the Famous Five"[8]. Growing up, learning about Emily Murphy, I also learned about the fact that she was part of advocating for the sterilization of Indigenous women and women with disabilities.

Modern forms of sterilization still happen in our communities. There hasn't been very much work of inquiry into the effects of those sterilizations on our communities, and other communities in Alberta, and I also don't think there is enough visibility on the fact that sterilization continues to occur in countries like Canada, for Indigenous women, and for women with disabilities, in the modern forms of reproductive control and contraceptions like the over-prescription of Depo-Provera to Indigenous youth, which has been proven to cause signs of infertility when over-used. So, while sterilization might not look like what it looked like with the Alberta Sterilization Act, there's new forms of sterilization still expanding. What does it

---

[7] Shantz, Jeff & PJ Lilley. 2005. "Putting the Control Back in Birth Control: Racism, Class and Reproductive Rights" in *The Northeastern Anarchist* (#10). Published by NEFAC (now Common Struggle). See it at http://jeffshantz.ca/node/8

[8] 'The Famous Five' are taught in public schools, as according to Wikipedia: "Canadian women who asked the Supreme Court of Canada to answer the question, 'Does the word 'Persons' in Section 24 of the British North America Act, 1867, include female persons?' ... The five women created a petition to ask this question. They sought to have women legally considered persons so that women could be appointed to the Senate."— http://en.wikipedia.org/wiki/The_Famous_Five_(Canada)

mean to have increasing numbers of missing and murdered Indigenous women in regards to this issue?

PJ: Also the forced sterilization of workers continues. We saw in our research, that over the years there has been a large increase in the number of factory workers that are offered (in a practically mandatory way) birth control pills each morning. This is especially prevalent (but not limited to) within "export processing zones" where there are high concentrations of displaced young women being exploited for long hours with low pay. So many other "hot zones" where environmental class repression is widespread, the rates of infant mortality also significantly higher. Like in Detroit, the infant mortality rate, especially for black children, was and still is appalling. So many people across the river in Windsor are affected with respiratory problems, especially recently with the Koch brothers Carbon company storing vast piles of petcoke along the river.

On a tangent here, I wanted to ask you: why the loon? The character seems to reappear in several different pieces.

EMK: The loon has a lot of sentimental significance to me in terms of an animal in my life. For my mom's side, which is my Indigenous side of my identity, the loon has been a really important animal; though I don't really use animals much in my images, I did use a porcupine recently, but it was also because I dequilled a porcupine for the first time, with my mom, which was ...

PJ: difficult?

EMK: Definitely difficult. *laughs* Loons are a solitary animal and if there are changes in the environment, loons are easily impacted. If there's a change in the environment in the ecosystem at all, they're the animals that don't do well with a lot of destruction, damage to the environment, or noise or people around.

"End the Prison Industrial Complex :
Prison(ers) on the land". December 2011.

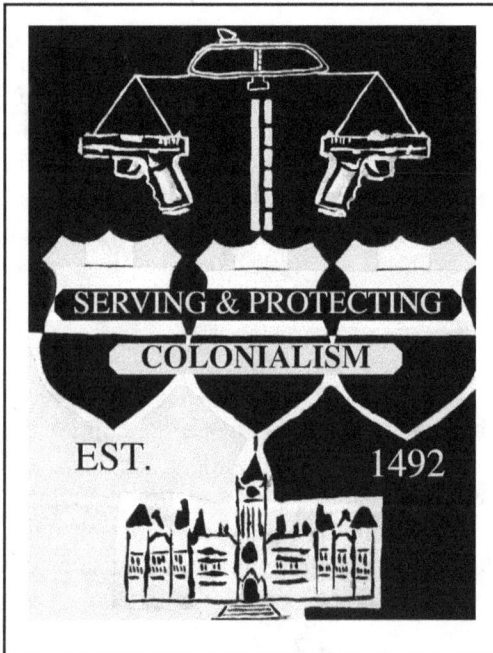

◄ "On
Policing"
for the Families
of Sisters in
Spirit + Native
Youth
Sexual Health
Network Joint
Statement:
"Responding
Together to
Change the
Story"

(June 2013)

PJ: I wanted to ask about the masked Warrior, she reappears with colorful variations, where is she from/what is she doing?

"Indigenous Womyn Warrior". Stencil series, Feb. 2012.

EMK: This one is interesting for this journal issue too, around the themes of terrorism and who gets called a terrorist. This one was done reflecting themes around the Canadian government's spying on Cindy Blackstock. I remember people saying "how could they spy on Cindy Blackstock?? She's just this gentle woman with this big heart." And I'm like, "Have you ever met Cindy Blackstock? That woman is dismantling the state one day at a time! She's a wicked warrior!" But, because she does work with kids, she's not a serious enough warrior?! No.

PJ: Yes, I've heard very similar expressions, it's true.

EMK: Yep, saying such is setting this precedent about what's taken seriously as activism, what is 'taking on the state.' But for me, it's about taking seriously the work that she's defending. She's literally keeping children in their communities, that's the work that she's doing, and if that isn't one of the most important things for us to defend in our communities, just as much as defending the land, then I'm not sure what the state could be more scared of! Removing children from their communities is a central part of the state's assimilation strategy.

PJ: So the womyn, wearing a mask, she's in action?

EMK: Yes, she is. It was actually done of a young, Indigenous woman, a Mohawk. We were talking of the Oka crisis as well... the use of military force (the tanks against her). She's Bear Clan, so that's where the bears come from, looking at those visual representations of the state vs. Indigenous peoples. It also has reference to Indigenous women leading the defense of land.

PJ: Another series that was quite striking is the 'Oral Warrior' women. Can I ask if that's a dental dam?   ▶

"Warrior Mask Re-imagined" or "Languages are spoken even when there are no words."
April 2012.

EMK: Yes, that's it exactly. I try and incorporate some of my sexuality in my artwork as well, but this piece goes back to that serious sense of the fact that we're losing our languages. I take that very seriously. I don't speak my Indigenous language, I can only really introduce myself, like many Indigenous youth. Only 2% of Métis people that speak their languages are left, although Cree is much more strong here in Alberta. It was also inspired by the sense that there are other ways that we can "practice" orally that are just as serious... while trying to lighten the mood about that, saying there's other ways that orally we can protect our world views and one of them is through safe oral sex, that we can be warriors through that way, without necessarily using words.

This next one was done around work that we were doing with midwives at the time, speaking about how within many of our communities midwives are traditional, but they've been criminalized. It's definitely a process that's about resistance and building up self-determination for our communities, and so there's reasons why the state forbids certain midwifery practices in hospitals. Building and reclaiming midwifery knowledge in Indigenous communities means that those who are pregnancy don't have to leave their community (and their supports) to give birth. ▼

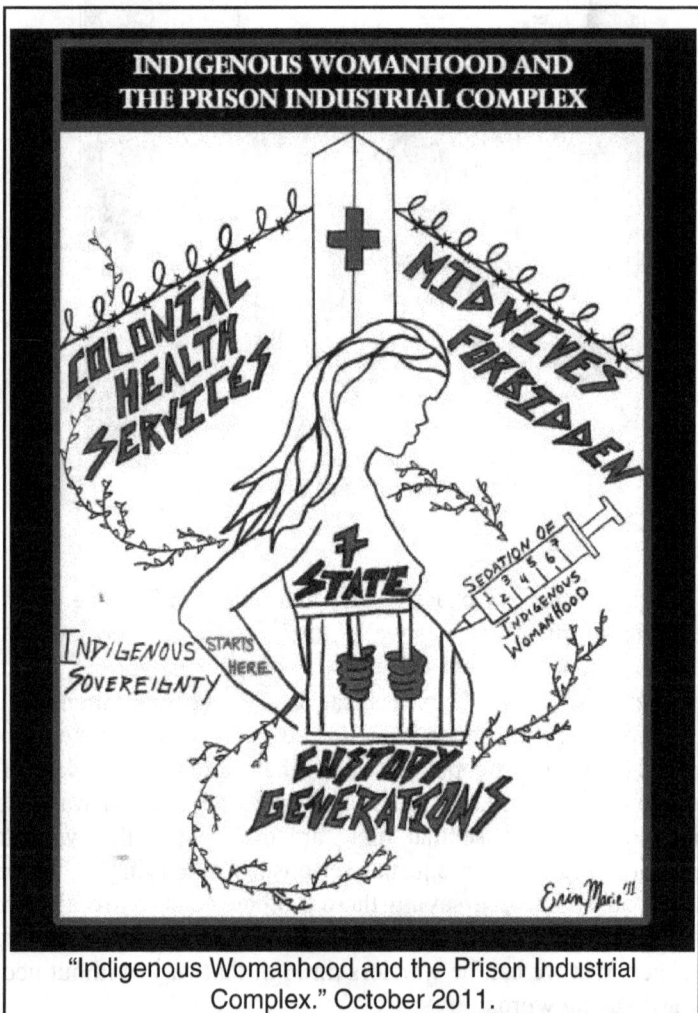

"Indigenous Womanhood and the Prison Industrial Complex." October 2011.

PJ: What about this *"Terra Nullius* -- Doctrine of Discovery" piece, when was that created?

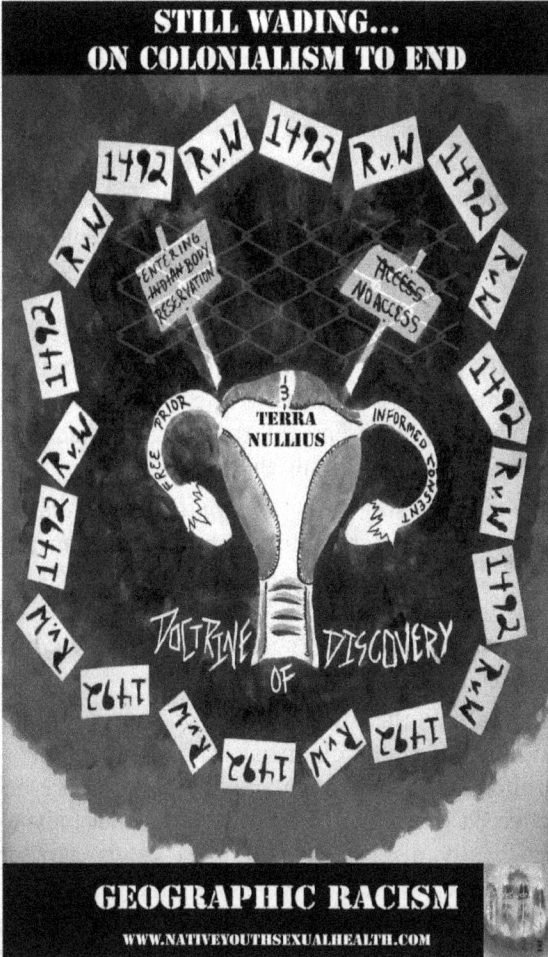

EMK: That was done for the Roe V. Wade 40th Anniversary... because abortion "rights"—in terms of asserting our rights to self-determination of our bodies—these are obviously not only 40 years old. We are not '*Terra Nullius*'.

Excerpt from "The Doctrine of Discovery is less of a problem than *terra nullius*"

"What made the Doctrine of Discovery so devastating was the application of a related legal concept, the principle of *terra nullius*. *Terra nullius* is a legal theory, or more accurately a legal fiction (something which may not be true, but is assumed to be so in order to facilitate particular legal findings) which holds that 'discovered' lands were, or are, empty. As a result of this 'emptiness', European powers asserted a unilateral right to simply take territories and resources within their jurisdictions. To put it another way, the legal fiction of *terra nullius* allowed European powers to simply assume that the underlying title to the entire territory belonged to those powers, rather than to the indigenous nations actually living there.

In a territory subject to *terra nullius*, once that territory has been properly claimed by a European power (vis a vis other powers), it would be assumed to be 'owned' by the power. By default, all lands, territories and resources would be the patrimony of the colonizing power.

This is important because the fundamental point of an indigenous rights claim is that indigenous peoples controlled lands, territories and resources before being 'discovered' by a European power and that they were never legally dispossessed of those lands, territories and resources. In other words, an indigenous rights case is, at base, a challenge to the assertion by the state that it has complete control over the lands, territories and resources within its international boundaries."

by the ***Reconciliation Project***, July 16, 2012:
(http://reconciliationproject.ca/2012/07/16/
the-doctrine-of-discovery-is-less-of-a-
problem-than-terra-nullius/)

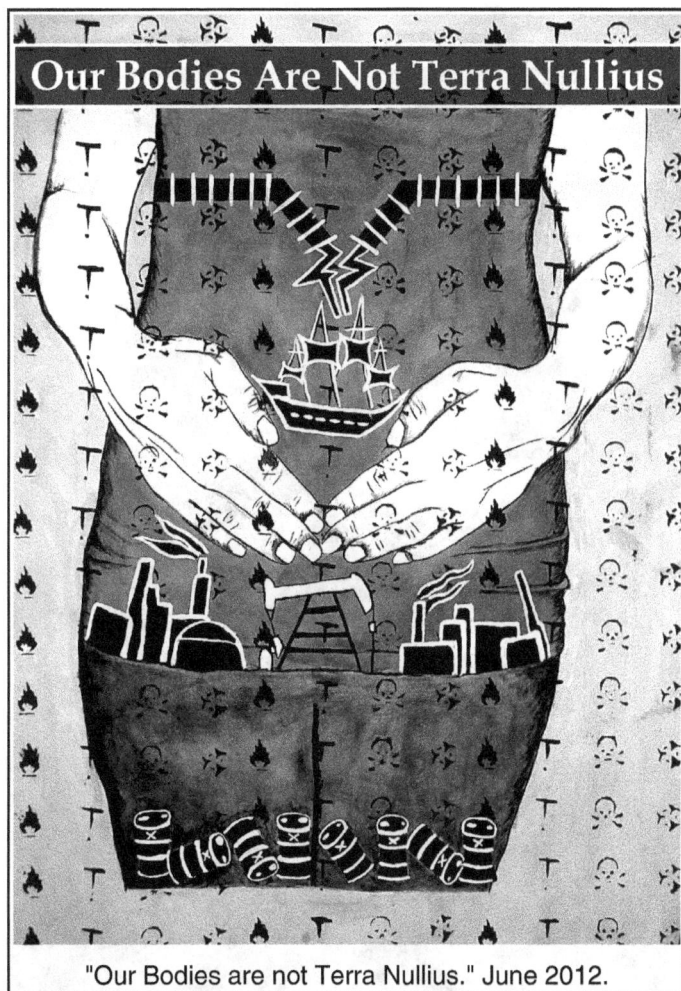

"Our Bodies are not Terra Nullius." June 2012.

▲ This piece was created as a political statement around the impacts of *terra nullius* (empty land, empty bodies) to be conquered. In this image the body is the territory that is represented as *terra nullius* and how experiences of environmental violence transfer to our bodies. It resists the idea that our bodies are *terra nullius*, while simultaneously resisting that Indigenous territories are *terra nullius*. From an Indigenous Feminist perspective, resistance to violent legal frameworks (such as *terra nullius*) can be taken up when we fight for the self-determination of our bodies as Indigenous Peoples.

"(de)colonize justice. listen to the land."
(December, 2011)

POLICE (IN)JUSTICE: RESPONDING TOGETHER TO CHANGE THE STORY

POLICE LINE DO NOT CROSS - DO NOT BE INDIGENOUS

DO NOT BE INDIGENOUS

DO NOT BE INDIGENOUS

DO NOT BE INDIGENOUS

DO NOT BE

"The Royal Canadian Mounted Police was originally created to control and manage the 'Indian Problem', which included using force, violence and coercion against our peoples. This is the RCMP's living legacy." Families of Sisters in Spirit

POLICE LINE DO NOT CROSS - DO NOT BE INDIGENOUS

ON OUR COVER...

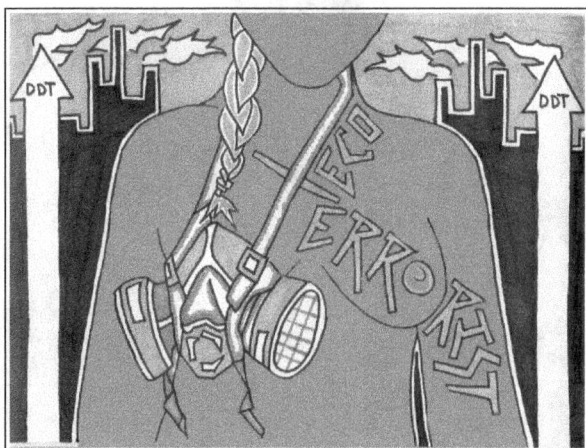

"Who is the Eco-Terrorist?
Defending food sovereignty"

'This piece of artwork is a response to
the increasing leadership of Indigenous
women who are standing up against
environmental violence, yet are labeled
as terrorists for defending land, bodies,
and future generations.'

(July 2013. 8.5 x 11, Sharpies.)
Original for Issue #2:
Radical Criminology
- ISBN: 0615877575 -

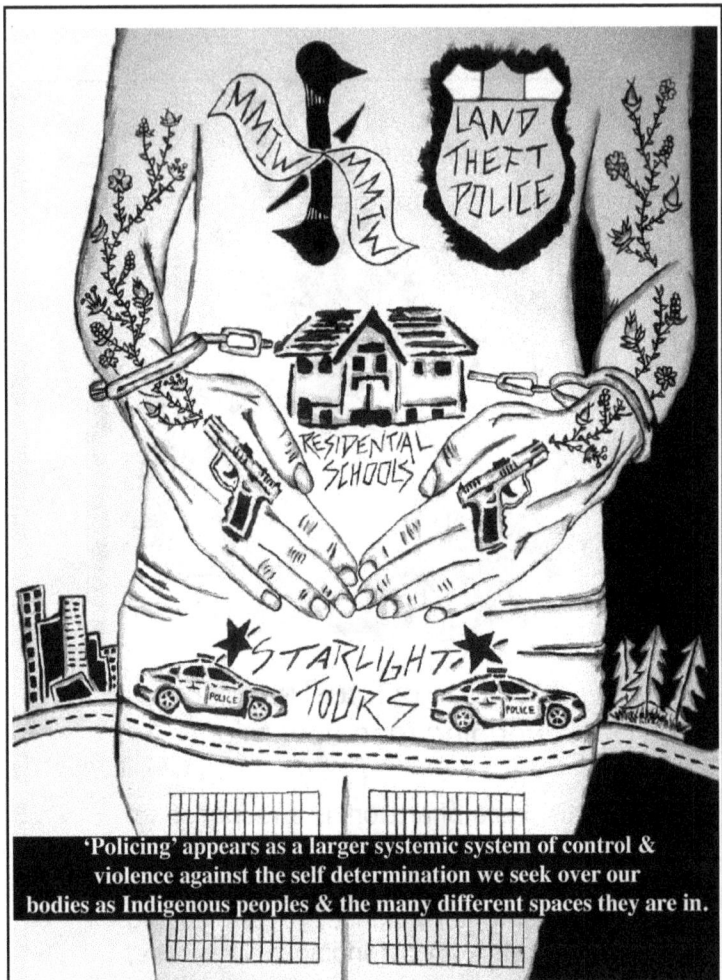

"On Policing"
for the Families of Sisters in Spirit &
Native Youth Sexual Health Network
Joint Statement: "Responding Together to Change the Story"
(June 2013)

FAMILIES OF SISTERS IN SPIRIT (FSIS)

is a grassroots volunteer organization led by families
of missing and murdered Indigenous women and girls,
with support from Indigenous and settler friends, allies,
and community organizations.

WWW.FAMILIESOFSISTERSINSPIRIT.COM

◀ After the release of the *Human Rights Watch* report; "Those
Who Take Us Away: Abusive Policing and Failures in
Protection of Indigenous Women and Girls in Northern British
Columbia", FSIS & the Native Youth Sexual Health Network
released a collaborative statement: "Police (In)Justice:
Responding Together to Change the Story".[9]

---

[9] See it at http://www.nativeyouthsexualhealth.com/
policeinjusticerespondingtogethertochangethestory.pdf

NATIVE YOUTH SEXUAL HEALTH NETWORK
AND INTERNATIONAL INDIAN TREATY COUNCIL:
JOINT STATEMENT PRESENTED AT THE 6TH SESSION OF THE
EXPERT MECHANISM ON THE RIGHTS OF INDIGENOUS PEOPLES
(EMRIP) JULY 8-12, 2013 [10]

For the purpose of this statement we are concentrating on the follow-up report on Indigenous Peoples and the right to participate in decision making with a focus on extractive industries and growing concerns expressed by Indigenous women regarding impacts to reproductive health and justice as well as issues of sexual violence impacting, in particular, Indigenous women, youth and children.

Our statement is also meant to inform the EMRIP study on the intersections of environmental and reproductive justice for this year's theme. We specifically see our sexual and reproductive health impacted by direct environmental violence resulting from violations of free, prior and informed consent, and an overburden of its effects is carried by Indigenous women, youth, and children. This results in a reflective need for reproductive and environmental justice.

To date, we recognize and appreciate the important work of the EMRIP on this topic, but also feel that there has not been sufficient focus from the reports of the EMRIP on the link between extractive industries and environmental violence, as well as sexual violence and exploitation. Environmental violence has particular effects on the health of Indigenous women, girls, and our generations yet unborn.

We reaffirm paragraph 37 of the follow-up report regarding Indigenous women and girls right to participate in decision making in the context of extractive industries as well as Article 22 of the UN Declaration regarding violence against Indigenous women and girls.

We acknowledge the terminology of environmental violence that was first articulated at the UN Permanent Forum's Interna-

---

[10] http:// www.nativeyouthsexualhealth.com/emrip2013item4.pdf

tional Expert Group Meeting on Combating Violence against Indigenous Women and Girls in January 2012. Environmental violence was raised by the International Indian Treaty Council as a specific manifestation of violence in this report addressing the devastating health and reproductive impacts to women, children, and future generations due to environmental toxins such as pesticides, mercury, nuclear contamination, and mining runoffs that are released into the environment without regard for the severe and ongoing harm.

The particular effects of environmental violence relating to impacts of extractive industries that we feel EMRIP, Indigenous human rights mechanisms and Member States need to address include:

-high rates of sexual, domestic, and family violence as well as sexual exploitation in Indigenous communities where extractive industries are taking place, usually accompanied by large numbers of miners or other workers from outside

-high rates of HIV and other sexually transmitted infections

-effects of contamination including mercury, uranium, and other toxins that continue to affect Indigenous women's reproductive health, their children, and generations unborn

Many of the women participating in the 1st and 2nd International Indigenous Women's Symposiums on Environmental and Reproductive Health in 2010 and 2012 presented testimony about the relationship of extractive industries, violence, and sexual exploitation as well as environmental contamination impacting reproductive health. We recognize that more work needs to be done to document these connections and impacts and request guidance from the EMRIP as to how these critical issues can be addressed in the context of their Study which has been submitted to the Human Rights Council and look forward to reporting back from the next global symposium, which will be held in Nicaragua in 2014.

NATIVE YOUTH SEXUAL HEALTH NETWORK: {ADDITIONAL NOTES TO THE} STUDY ON ACCESS TO JUSTICE IN THE PROMOTION AND PROTECTION OF THE RIGHTS OF INDIGENOUS PEOPLES[11]

We are presenting information to supplement the study on access to justice in the promotion and protection of the rights of Indigenous Peoples. On this item, we present information and recommendations that expand on the justice report to include effects of structural and institutional discrimination regarding the intersection of justice with sexual and reproductive health and rights.

Within the region of North America, Indigenous youth are disproportionately affected by HIV through increases in our HIV infection rates, and lack of access to culturally safe health care. For example, in Canada between 1998 and the end of 2006, nearly one-third (32.4%) of Aboriginal people diagnosed with HIV were under the age of 30.[12]

Compounded with this health crisis, is the issue of criminalization, which targets Indigenous youth for high rates of incarceration due to racism and the legacy of colonialism within the justice system itself. Racial profiling and police violence are still very much a reality for Indigenous youth across North America, which should also be taken into consideration with the well-documented high rates of sexual violence for Indigenous women.

While Indigenous youth in Canada represent 6% of the general youth population, they account for 26% of youth admitted to correctional services.[13] Furthermore, Indigenous young women comprise 36% of all young women incarcerated. American Indian and Alaska Native youth are arrested at a rate of 3 times the national average, and 79% of youth in the Federal Bureau of

---

[11] Presented at the 6th session of the Expert Mechanism on the Rights of Indigenous Peoples July 8-12, 2013; Available at:
http://www.nativeyouthsexualhealth.com/emrip2013item5.pdf

[12] Population Specific HIV/AIDS Status Report: Aboriginal Peoples, Public Health Agency of Canada (PHAC), 2010 http://www.phac-aspc.gc.ca/aids-sida/publication/ps-pd/aboriginal-autochtones/index-eng.php

[13] Canadian Centre for Justice Statistics. 2012. "Youth correctional statistics in Canada, 2011/2012." Statistics Canada: Government of Canada.

Prison's custody are American Indian and Alaska Native.[14] Overall, Indigenous peoples now account for 21.5 per cent of prison population in Canada despite being only 4% of the general population.[15]

These interactions with the justice system start young with Indigenous children still being removed from families and communities by child welfare agencies due to poverty, racism, and structural issues within the system which has historically labeled Indigenous families and mothers as "unfit". These realities are even worse for Two Spirit and transgender youth who experience even more targeting by police, as well as discrimination inside and outside the criminal justice system.

A further intersection of the issue of justice is the criminalization of HIV. This involves serious criminal charges being brought onto people living with HIV even in circumstances where HIV was not transmitted and protection such as a condom was used. This does nothing to stop HIV infection and in fact creates an environment of fear and stigma that prevents effective public health efforts like testing for sexually transmitted infections and public education.[16] Increased criminalization in fact endangers the lives of people living with HIV especially women in abusive relationships. Furthermore, with no harm reduction services like clean syringes and a lack of equitable health care for those who are incarcerated, HIV and Hepatitis C are on a significant rise in prisons, where Indigenous peoples sexual and reproductive rights are already routinely violated; including the shackling of pregnant women also while in labor, coerced sterilization and sexual violence from prison staff and guards.

Already youth labeled as "young offenders" in Canada and the US are now facing mandatory minimum sentencing as well as stricter and tougher sentences for minor drug offenses with-

---

[14] American Indians and Crime: A BJS Statistical Profile, 2004. http://www.bjs.gov/content/pub/pdf/aic02.pdf

[15] Troian, Martha. 2013."Warehousing Indigenous Women: The story of Kinew James, an indigenous woman who died in a Canadian prison". CBC: Manitoba . http://www.cbc.ca/manitoba/features/warehousing/

[16] Canadian HIV/AIDS Legal Network & Global Network of People Living with HIV. (2010). Criminalization of HIV Exposure: Canada. http://www.aidslaw.ca/EN/lawyers-kit/documents/Canadianlaw.pdf

out an increase in community based restorative justice, and in fact cuts to Indigenous cultural practices within correctional services. Additionally, this is actually in contravention of a previous Supreme Court ruling *"Gladue"* in Canada that mandated judges taking into account the history of colonization when it came to sentencing Aboriginal people. Sound evidence has already been documented that increased criminalization and incarceration do not actually produce more safety and well-being in communities.

Out of all of these realities as they pertain to accessing justice, we recommend the following:

> 1. That the criminalization of HIV be included in an extension of EMRIP's study on access to justice with a focus on Indigenous women and youth, as well as legal standards and prosecutorial guidelines that are culturally safe for Indigenous peoples;

> 2. That UN agencies and Member States continue to seriously consider Indigenous methods of accountability and justice, including restorative justice models that include the full, effective and meaningful participation and leadership of Indigenous youth

> 3. In addition to "expert" advice from UN agencies and member states, we recommend future EMRIP studies take into account the lived realities of Indigenous Peoples, especially youth, who have experience with police violence, criminalization and incarceration - in particular the rights, health, and well being for Indigenous peoples who are currently imprisoned.

We can do more than just react to the harms of injustices; we can restore, we can create, and we can grow stronger together.

ADDITIONAL RESOURCES:

Canadian Aboriginal AIDS Network. (2006). Aboriginal People and Incarceration Issues related to HIV/AIDS, Hepatitis C and Residential Schooling.

"Marginalized: Aboriginal Women's Experiences in Federal Corrections." http://www.publicsafety.gc.ca/res/cor/apc/_fl/apc-33-eng.pdf

"Police (In)Justice: Responding Together to Change the Story." *Collaborative Statement and Resources*: Native Youth Sexual Health Network & Families of Sisters in Spirit. http://www.nativeyouthsexualhealth.com/policeinjusticerespondingtogeth ertochangethestory.pdf

Globalization and the Politics of Culture: An Interview with Imre Szeman

BY *MARC JAMES LÉGER*[1]

What is the role of culture in an era of globalization? This is one of the questions that animates the work of Imre Szeman, founder of the Canadian Association of Cultural Studies and Canada Research Chair in Cultural Studies at the University of Alberta. Szeman's thinking combines a strong appreciation of the critical potential of cultural studies work with an understanding of the importance of Marxist theory, especially at this critical moment in human history. With the end of national culture as a framework for progress in the arts, culture becomes increasingly tied to the new master narrative, he says, of the traumas of globalization. As culture's agenda is increasingly set by the operations of global capital, it becomes imperative, he argues, to create an imaginative vocabulary that can challenge biocapitalism's fantasy of endless accumulation. While globalization democratizes the imagination, creating new identities and new public spheres, for Szeman, it simultaneously shifts our focus away from culture—the predominant aesthetic and representational condition of postmodernism—towards macropolitical issues. In this context, he says, class struggle reasserts itself, political economy returns with a vengeance, and even the immanent aesthetic of workerist theory seems to pale in comparison with the transcendent mediation of radical contestation.

---

[1] Marc James Léger is an artist, writer and educator living in Montreal. He has published many essays in cultural theory, including contributions to *Afterimage, Art Journal, Creative Industries Journal, Etc, Fuse, Inter, Journal of Aesthetics and Protest*, and *Third Text*. He is editor of *Culture and Contestation in the New Century* (Intellect, 2011) and author of *Brave New Avant Garde: Essays in Contemporary Art and Politics* (Zero Books, 2012).

Whereas the theorists of empire, Michael Hardt and Antonio Negri, argue that desire must become practical, that joyful communitarianism must of necessity replace the "fanatical ethical purity" of revolutionary theory, Szeman emphasizes the fact that this immediacy of desire is largely a result of biopolitical cultural production, which, while it causes a mutation of capitalism, is nevertheless fueled by older, basic processes of resource extraction and the industrial exploitation of wage labor. If globalization implies that culture's relative autonomy is unsustainable, Szeman proposes that we should fight to win spaces of autonomy, that revolution holds more promise for us than the evolutionary anti-art of exodus. Against the fetishization of theoretical novelty, Szeman therefore suggests that the imaginative resources of cultural resistance are readily at hand and all it takes for us to imagine an after to globalization is the return to a strategic realism that is willing to confront the limitations and arbitrariness of neoliberal economics.

After a lecture he gave in Montreal in March 2011, I asked Imre for an interview, the outcome of which produced more questions and more topics than we could reasonably manage in one text. Over the summer months we corresponded over email and he kindly endeavored to provide responses to a few questions.

Marc James Léger: In your essay "Imagining the Future: Globalization, Postmodernism and Criticism," you argue that the idea of the artist as a vanguard is definitely over and that this is a good thing. Art and politics proceed today with uncertainty, you say. I was particularly interested in this essay with the simple way that you contrast postmodernism with globalization. Globalization is less about aesthetics and cultural representation and has more to do with an agenda set for culture by global capital. Could you tell us how it is that you came up with this solution to post-postmodernism? Also, could you say more about this predominance of capitalist globalization and what you might say to a thinker like Nicolas Bourriaud who is eager to ask, well, what then is the mode of aesthetics that corresponds to this new era? I wonder if you think there is any space for an avant-garde articulation of culture in this context.

Imre Szeman: The relationship between art and politics is indeed uncertain—or so it seems to me. The gestures of many of those art works (and artists) explicitly committed to political engagement and change are towards little more than simply difference from the present rather than some (aesthetically or politically) well-articulated interrogation of system and structure. In art as in other areas of our social life, we exist at a moment in which political ideas adequate to the present are in short supply. Despite all manner of social inequality and political obscenities done in the name of democracy, a broad swathe of the planet's population has come to accept that the primary function of the state is to run itself out of business. After 2008, neoliberalism exists less as ideology than as habit—an increasingly common ready-to-hand vocabulary of quotidian complaint about public waste that supposedly can only be cured by private pragmatism, whatever the consequences to public life. The inadequacies of the state as a result of the reduction of its services only confirms the veracity of this social narrative—a closed spiral of cause and effect that has proven to be enormously difficult to challenge or unsettle.

I don't need to rehearse the now long and persistent attacks that have been carried out on the idea or ideal of the avant garde that lent to the practice of art a revolutionary potential. The collapse of the autonomy of art as a result of the expansion of mass culture—a process described authoritatively by Peter Bürger—is viewed by some critics as cause for alarm and by others as no big deal. The alarm? Only through its relative autonomy from capitalism could art offer a challenge to it. However, this very possibility tended to occlude the fact that its autonomy left it always already separate from the quotidian in a manner that meant it could not truly intervene in capitalist culture. There is still another response to this configuration of the power of art, which is to view the original formulae by which art is assigned its potentially powerful autonomy as something like a category mistake, which is why its eclipse is seen as no big deal. This is certainly true of the work of Pierre Bourdieu, for whom aesthetic judgment acts as a euphemism that underwrites and enables social distinctions, and little more. It is true, too, of Jacques Rancière's intervention into the relationship between aesthetics and politics, which reconfigures it in yet another way: art as a specific form of work on the "distribution of the sensible," a field in which politics proper acts as well. The rupture or break once associated with vanguardist imaginings of the aesthetic are in this schema muted, to say the least. In *The Politics of Aesthetics*, for instance, Rancière writes,

> the arts only ever lend to projects of domination or emancipation what they are able to lend them, that is to say, quite simply, what they have in common with them: bodily positions and movements, functions of speech, parceling out of the visible and the invisible. Furthermore, the autonomy they can enjoy or the subversion they can claim credit for rest on the same foundation. (19)

To me this view is not so far removed from the "relational aesthetics" championed by Nicolas Bourriaud, though he lacks anything like the politico-aesthetic structure Rancière has elaborated around visibility/sensibility and equality. I'm inclined to agree with Hal Foster's critique that Bourriaud's aesthetics amounts to little more than a "shaky analogy between an open work and an inclusive society, as if a desultory form might evoke a democratic community, or a non-hierarchical installation predict an egalitarian world" (193).

I have a slightly different take on the eclipse of artist as a vanguard. If Bourdieu sees the politics hitherto associated with the aesthetic as bad sociology and Rancière views it as something akin to sloppy political philosophy, what strikes me with especial force are the impacts of historical shifts in dominant discourses on the social significance of art and aesthetics. In "Imagining the Future," several things emerge from a comparison of postmodernism and globalization as dominant narratives. The postmodern was an aesthetic category before it became a larger descriptor of an epistemic or ontological condition. Globalization, on the other hand, seems to have little to do with culture or aesthetics *per se*. When one says 'global culture' it is to affirm the realities that postmodernism only hinted at rather than to name a specific artistic or architectural mode or style. With globalization, the emphasis is directly on the restructuring of relations of politics and power, on the rescaling of economic production from the national to the transnational, on the light speed operations of finance capital, and on the societal impacts of the explosive spread of information technologies—no need for any complex symptomatology!   Finally, globalization is a dominant discourse with a much stronger public presence than postmodernism. Social and political struggles occur over the ideologies and imperatives of globalization in a way that they never did in postmodernism—more is at stake, and more directly so. One of things that I argue for in "Imagining the Future" and elsewhere is that this shift in dominant social narratives away from culture to a blunter, cruder argument about the nature of power is a sign of an evacuation of the power of art and culture. Dominance once required an investment in the practices and discourses of art and culture, including the humanities in universities; now power seems less anxious about having a purchase on this terrain—it's no longer where power is lived and consolidated. This has to do, of course, with social and technological developments that have led to a commodification of images, which is, in the words of Fredric Jameson, "why it is vain to expect a negation of the logic of the commodity production from it" (135), as well as the different relationship to culture generated by mass culture—a development narrated by many thinkers, from Guy Debord to Jameson himself.

Does this mean that art and cultural production once had a power that has completely evaporated in the context of globalization? This is how many critics seem to read the situation. But isn't this to fix art at a specific moment in time—an avantgarde moment whose politics are already in question in any case? Doesn't art, too, change in conjunction with broader social developments? Mikkel Bolt Rasmussen has recently suggested that while much art practice remains complicit with established powers, "at the same time it is important to point out that the space of art is still characterized by the presence of various representations of the political and attempts to use the field of art as a starting point for the visualization of conflicts that have been marginalized in the broader mainstream public sphere" (199). It's a mistake to write off the political possibilities of art; it's a mistake, too, to imagine it to be more than a sideshow in the ebb and flow of global capital—that is, as a site at which one might expect wholesale political change. It might seem a banal point, but it has to be made: it's 2011, not 1911.

MJL: Indeed, it's not 1911 and by all accounts we're in a world of biopolitical governance. However, I completely agree with

Alain Badiou when he argues that certain sequences and events
cannot be limited to specific dates—for example, the idea that
communism died a very certain death in 1989. A specific sequence has come to a close but this does not condemn us to a
post-traumatic complicity either. We can have anxieties about
affirmative culture or about recuperation but that's not all there
is. One can look at this in very pragmatic terms to say that so-
cialism is not something that exists only in China and Cuba, but
that many social programs, environmental and labor regulations
that we benefit from here in Canada are the products of socialist
ideas and endeavors. By the same token, if autonomous art has
been falsely sublated into culture industry, as Bürger says, we
can nevertheless find avant-garde forms of resistance to capitalist domination that are not on the same order as the postmodern
politics of representation. I wouldn't say "good riddance" to
the idea of the avant-garde anymore than I would say it to the
idea of communism. And if there is to be an after to capitalist
globalization, I can't personally imagine how Marx wouldn't
have something to do with getting there.

   In terms of what I wanted to bring up with regard to
Bourriaud's idea of the "altermodern," what I meant to ask you
about is the eagerness with which cultural theorists may want to
wish   away   the   problems   associated   with   economic
globalization, least of all its implications for neoliberal policy,
and brings the focus back to culture. The particular form that
this takes today is that of variations on the idea of pluralism:
difference,   hybridity,   transnationalism,   multiculturalism,
diaspora, cosmopolitanism. In the same essay, "Imagining the
Future," you argue that the agenda that is set for culture is
informed by the operations of global capital and that this has
become a new master narrative. Is the culturalization of
politics that one finds in postmodern discourse in any way
challenged by the return to political economy and class
analysis? By the way, I don't think that Bourdieu thought that
politics associated with aesthetic ideology was bad sociology,
but rather the outcome of a particular class habitus, which had
to do with his appreciation of the concept of totality. As I see
things what we have today is an ascendance of petty bourgeois
allodoxia in which the lifestyle concerns of an international
class refuses all determinations in matters of identity and so we

have a clear shift from national culture to global petty bourgeois culture.

IS: I don't think that anything I suggested above means "good riddance"! Questioning the specific politico-aesthetic configuration associated with the historical avant garde is intended to get us past a (still, it must be said) widely held feeling that the connection between art and politics is over and done with——over and done with because it is thought to be able to operate in a certain way (now gone) and no other. I agree: this doesn't mean we have to wallow in the certitudes of affirmative culture. It does mean, however, that we have to address new circumstances head on.

With respect to the focus on culture in contemporary thought, there are two related but importantly different claims being made here. The first has to do with a focus on culture as opposed to analyses of political economy or class; the second asks a question about the nature of that focus—what you here describe correctly as variations on ideas about the importance of pluralism. I don't think one can avoid assessments and analyses of everything that constitutes 'culture.' The social world is legible only through the discourses and narratives that constitute it. Capitalism is one of these, as are, say, the varied discourses of governmentality that comprise the 'rational' and efficient organization of populations at the present time. This is not to say that all cultural or social discourses operate with equal force or importance, or that some cluster of them shouldn't be taken as a politico-social axiomatic that offers a key to what is happening to us now. But nor is it to say that those elements determined to be axiomatic are plainly and clearly the dominant site of power 'in the last instance'—the kind of idea that legitimates reductive or vulgar analyses of all kinds. We sometimes forget why there was a cultural turn in the first place, which has to do with the reshaping of everyday life in the context of mass culture and new technologies of communication and information, and the consequent impact of this turn on epistemologies and ontologies of the social and political. *Nothing* social or political is given immediately to sensation; we have to comprehend it through the web of desires, beliefs, information and affect that constitutes 'culture' today. If this is the case, we can't possibly avoid thinking about culture.

My objection is that as important as culture is, there is also a tendency of cultural theorists to overvalue it—to not even be tempted to vulgarly assert the significance of economics or political structure, since they don't recognize the importance of these factors for culture to begin with, and because their concern begins and starts with cultural objects whose significance for analyses is framed not by a problem to be solved, but by traditions of analysis within institutions of higher education. The pressures and politics of the latter also tend to generate analyses that have to place novelty or innovation at the heart of critical writing—the discernment in this or that piece of fiction or work of art of, for instance, the secret to the entire system of capitalism, or just as frequently, of a model of political engagement one doesn't find in the world at large. The impact of culture on social epistemologies doesn't mean that one should wallow in culture, or that knowledge as such is now impossible (as one variant of postmodernism suggests), but that our sense of the world and its operations have of necessity to be complex and multi-layered.

As to the second point: insofar as hybridity, transnationalism, multiculturalism, diaspora, etc., draw attention to the operations of power vis-à-vis the management of difference, the shaping of populations through movement in space (or the prevention of such movement), impediments to social possibility and mobility due to cultural, social, and racial differences, etc., these are valuable concepts with which to understand globalization. My anxiety is that often enough such concepts are deployed in the absence of an analysis of the operations of identity and difference *within* capitalism; such a politics as does exist is often unreflexively liberal, connected mainly to the dynamics of political and social tolerance and the extension of rights but without a larger consideration of the imperatives of global capital. As long as it can extract surplus, difference isn't a problem for capital (though it obviously is for the older formations of nation and nationalism). Indeed, as many critics have pointed out, pluralism and difference are today powerful ideas guiding and organizing the practices of consumption and consumerism.

I wouldn't bundle 'cosmopolitanism' into these pluralistic terms. The criticisms of cosmopolitanism tend to be that it *isn't* particularistic or pluralistic, but that in its presumed universalism it is far too limiting a concept. There are liberal cosmopolitanisms (such as Daniele Archibugi's) that see the concept as little more than the name for international political schemes that would address problems that are global rather than national in scale. Tim Brennan's suggestion that we can already take "contemporary neoliberal orthodoxy as a form of unofficial party organization across national frontiers" (42) is pretty much all one has to say in response to Archibugi's "cosmopolitical democracy project."

But it is possible to use cosmopolitanism as a powerful regulative and political ideal—as something akin to how equality works in Rancière's thought. This is, it seems to me, how it first appears in Immanuel Kant's "Perpetual Peace." The first two of the three definitive articles of perpetual peace echo Archibugi's aims by laying the groundwork for a formally instituted international body that would be the managing political organ of a federation of independent nation states, each established on the basis of a republican constitution (think today of the UN or IMF). The third and final definitive article ("Cosmopolitan Right Shall Be Limited to Conditions of Universal Hospitality") attempts to identify a right that all people should have everywhere—a *universal* right.   Universal hospitality means that a stranger who arrives on someone else's territory must be treated peaceably if they themselves are not hostile. The reason for this? Kant writes:

> All men are entitled to present themselves in the society of others by virtue of their right to communal possession of the earth's surface. Since the earth is a globe, they cannot disperse over an infinite area, but must necessarily tolerate one another's company. And no one originally has any greater right than anyone else to occupy any particular portion of the earth. The community of man is divided by uninhabitable parts of the earth's surface such as oceans and deserts, but even then, the *ship* or the *camel* (the ship of the desert) make it possible for them to approach their fellows over these ownerless tracts, and to utilize as a means of social intercourse that *right to the earth's surface* which the human race shares in common. (29)

This strikes me as an important and radical claim, and it is one
that seems to go against almost everything else that Kant writes
in "Perpetual Peace." The right to the earth's surface—a right
that necessitates universal hospitality for those crossing borders
—does not supersede the fact that claims *have been* made to
this or that patch of the earth, and that hospitality has to be
granted by owner to visitor, by citizen to foreigner. However
much in Kant's view nations might in the future be held together in an increasingly powerful international federation, under-
written by increasingly universal laws that apply to everyone,
the borders between nation states appear to remain fixed. At
times, Kant simply presumes the inevitable existence of nations; at other times, he argues for their necessity: nations can't
or shouldn't intermingle due to linguistic and religious differences produced by nature (through a kind of geographic deter-
minism); or nations shouldn't be brought under a single power,
because "laws progressively lose their impact as government
increases its range" (38). Nature separates humanity into nations, and does so, according to Kant, "wisely" because the
leader of a single earthly nation could only ever be a despot.
As a root universal principle, all of humanity can claim the
right to all of the globe; the reality of the situation—which is
seen by Kant less as something unfortunate than as a productive
and valuable state of affairs—is that borders create strangers,
and to strangers we owe little more than hospitality. If we take
cosmopolitanism to be the right to universal access, however, it
places a demand that a justification be made in every situation
where such access doesn't exist, a demand we can turn on Kant
himself. The articulation of a right to the earth's surface in the
same passage in which the universality of this right is undercut
by the assertion of a need to tolerate visitors goes to the heart of
the problems and limits of the liberal rights regimes that manage our legal and political affairs today.

   Can we not say that political art makes a similar demand,
engaging in a conceptual and political game that asks why *this*
and not *that*? It might not be a demand that is answered by society at large; it is important, however, that such demands
which pierce to the heart of the organization of power are made,
and, to bring it back around to where your question started, this

of necessity goes beyond the limits that still adhere to how we tend to understand 'culture.'

MJL: The problem with affirmative culture is not that one might wallow in it, it's rather, as I understand Adorno and Marcuse, that it allows us to forget suffering and at the same time it might also, as is evident in some forms of progressive culture, seek to satiate audiences with moral indignity and sentimentality without imparting any useful sense of how a situation could be subjectivized. In other words, the criticism of affirmative culture is not what it allows in terms of pleasure, it's what it doesn't allow in terms of equality, truth, justice. I tend to agree with your description of cosmopolitanism, though I am concerned to distinguish class politics from cosmopolitics, which promotes legal notions of human rights that act in tandem with the developmentalist aspects of economic globalization and military incursion. I think that it could be useful to propose a triangulation of culture, politics, and economy, and avoid what anarchist thought and media studies often do, which is, when speaking about culture and politics, to collapse social relations with means of production, or to assume that culture is directly political. This is to say that we should allow culture a certain measure of effectivity and even of autonomy with regard to both politics and economics.

What you say about hospitality relates in some ways to what I alluded to in terms of petty bourgeois allodoxia and biocapitalism. Progressives are enthralled at the moment with models of culture that propose various ways that social subjects should change their structures of feeling through affective bonding, stranger intimacy, tolerance towards the other and towards the stranger within ourselves, etc., with variations on ideas borrowed from Bergsonian models of creative evolution or Levinasian ethics which are then linked to various political agendas (anarchist, social democratic, liberal and even conservative). Most often these anti-revolutionary reformist models make use of very naive or idealist notions of social engineering that are not unlike counter-cultural models from the past decades and which typically exclude class analysis. This to me is an indication of the ascendance of petty bourgeois culture, as it's understood for example by Giorgio Agamben in his book *The Com-*

ing Community. The problem here is that in this cultural context left militancy is made to stand in for everything that is universalizing, masculinist, totalizing, and so on. This attitude tends to avoid complex uses of the notions of totality, rationality, subjectivity, and universality that are in fact necessary if we are to pursue a politics of universal emancipation.

With reference to what you discussed, an interesting example of critical public art is that of Christoph Schlingensief's *Bitte liebt Österreich!* (Please Love Austria!) of 2000.[2] The artist organized an outdoor "Big Brother" type reality show in which the Austrian public was asked to vote for which asylum seeker should be allowed to stay in the country and which should be deported. The participants were kept in a container camp that was marked *Ausländer Raus* (foreigners out!), which was meant to stage the popularity of extreme right-wing ideas in Austria and the state's recognition of the right populist FPÖ party of Jörg Haider. In many ways Schlingensief's work anticipated the recent violent acts of Anders Behring Breivik in Norway and the communication of sympathy for his ideas on behalf of neo-fascist groups in France and Italy, not to mention the exploitation by the mainstream media of anti-Muslim rhetoric. In less drastic terms, this also reflects public policies in Canada and the U.S. that are meant to detract from scrutiny of labor policy, industrial relations, and the like.

My next question then relates specifically to your essay "Marxist Literary Criticism, Then and Now," which was published in the journal *Mediations* in 2009. In this piece you state that there are three basic modes of Marxist art criticism: (1) reminders to historicize and to focus on class and political economy, (2) critiques of the institutions of cultural production and analysis, and (3) anxieties about affirmative culture and critique of the cultural studies tendency to find moments of resistance in almost anything. I'm wondering, with reference to your recent collaboration with Eric Cadzyn, *After Globalization*, if there is still some room within critical theory for the Marxist analysis of the transition to communism and also if there is anything left of the Marxist-Leninist-Maoist experiment with political organiz-

---

[2] **IMAGE (opposite):** Christoph Schlingensief, *Bitte liebt Österreich! (Please Love Austria)*, 2000. Performance event. Photo © David Baltzer/bildbuehne.de.

Christoph Schlingensief, Bitte liebt Österreich! (Please Love Austria), 2000. Performance event. Photo © David Baltzer/bildbuehne.de

ation. In other words, it seems to me that if class struggle is to reassert itself and if "political economy is back in style," which indeed it is, art criticism would have something to say about political organization. I ask this question knowing very well that in the contemporary "visual arts" at least there is enormous energy being dedicated to organization in relation to new class compositions. Most of this, however, tends to be devised in terms of utopian and small-scale anarchist models, which the international class of capitalists, the state bureaucracies and their military-police apparatuses are hardly worried about. How then can (2) spend less time worrying about (3) and do more to be useful to (1) and what do you think the role of cultural studies is in this age of post-politics, austerity capitalism, and the corporatization of the university?

IS: These are good points to make. Certain concepts come loaded with meanings that, as a result of their histories, cannot be easily shaken off. And so cosmopolitanism does speak to human rights regimes and developmental schema, even if at its core it names a possibility of affiliations and connections that go beyond national sentiment or the prohibitions of a lifeworld organized around property. As those theorists who draw attention to negative cosmopolitanisms make clear, all too often discourses of cosmopolitanism legitimate imperialistic and hegemonic intrusions by the powerful into spaces they want to manage and control. Narratives of human rights, of economic and social development, and (more lately) of globalization appeal to universalistic measures of the human *as such*, against which the state of this or that part of the world can be assessed. Given the imperatives and desires of the forces that are creating and promoting these measures, it comes as little surprise that the universalism they promote is suspect.

As for the effectivity and autonomy of culture: this, too, is a good point to make. If I tend to err in the other direction it is because culture is more often than not viewed as fully autonomous (in both critical thought and in society at large), and so reminders of limits, blocks, and conditions of possibility can't help but introduce important considerations into the discussions of the 'what' and 'why' of culture. And I take your point about the fear of notions such as totality and universality. As I said above, there's no question that appeals to universality made by some thinkers (for example, liberals such as Kwame Anthony

Appiah or Martha Nussbaum) have to be read with a critical eye. At the same time, a complete rejection of universality—as something akin to a category mistake when it comes to the rich diversity of human Being—is in fact a perverse affirmation of that universality which already exists: the universality of capitalist subjectivity. In an era that has been described as one in which the hitherto formal subsumption of labor under capital has become real, we already have a universal subject—an exploited subject, lacking in rights, who endures "the meaningless and alienating qualities of so many jobs and so much of daily life in the midst of immense but unevenly distributed potentiality for human flourishing" (Harvey).

Is there room for an analysis of a transition to communism? One hopes so. Is there anything left of experiments with political organization? There are. I think immediately of Erik Olin Wright's *Envisioning Real Utopias* (2010) as an example of a recent book that unapologetically devotes itself to framing emancipatory social possibilities, or of the 2006 documentary *The Power of Community: How Cuba Survived Peak Oil*, which examines the country's imaginative, collective response to the loss of more than half of its oil imports. Though it is perhaps too easy to be cynical about the significance of contemporary visual arts in its explorations of political organization, I agree with you that the visual arts *are* a site in which this issue of organizational possibility is being posed and examined. However the arts might be greeted by the capitalist class, however they might be contained and consigned to spaces of relative predictability, the conceptual experimentations of the visual arts remain a genuine resource—*especially* as so many artists and art collectives move beyond lingering modernist interrogations of the nature and subject of art, and simply enact scenarios and carry out social investigations to see what these might reveal or produce. I like Hal Foster's recent reading of the work of Thomas Hirschhorn, for instance. Foster sees Hirschhorn's work as consisting of explorations of precarity, expenditure, and of the conceptual difficulty of reading the present (the mode of the *bête* in Hirschhorn's work, who operates within the social circumstances of emergency); the resources Hirschhorn draws upon in doing so are those "that lie dormant in the 'general intellect' of the multitude, a multitude that, to different de-

grees, faces a state of emergency today" (Foster 2011: 105).
Here we have an artist engaged in an exploration of the fundamental problems of organization today: a socioeconomic system governed by fear and insecurity, as well as a helplessness
in the face of everything from the scale of existing infrastructure (from the military-security apparatus to our sheer dependence on technology) to looming ecological crises; a world
premised on narratives and fantasies of growth that will have to
re-build itself around perpetual lack; and finally, a historical
moment of confused epistemologies which are hurt rather than
helped by the enormous amounts of data we are so adept at generating. Foster describes Hirschhorn's use of everyday materials and techniques as the "search for a nonexclusive public, a
public after the apparent dissolution of the public sphere" (114).
That seems to be a good description of where many of us find
ourselves at the moment when it comes to confronting the problem of political organization.

The question you end with about cultural studies is a big
one. I refuse to write off the university, despite its many problems and limits. It remains a central site of knowledge production and legitimation; it is a space in which a large part of the
population in Western countries (and an increasingly large part
in the rest of the world: non-Western students now make up
more than half of the globe's university population) spends a
key point in their lives, a place in which the passage to (an
imagined) full citizenship takes place alongside an immersion
in social and political codes and beliefs. There are numerous
other sites at which such social pedagogy takes place—everywhere from the communications media to spaces of religion.
Still, the university matters, even if different parts of it might
matter to different degrees, and even if it is not the sole politi-
cal-social-cultural arbiter.

And so, in this context, is it not important to have an approach to culture that is (ideally) self-reflective about its practice as a mode of knowledge production (and indeed, clear
about the need to consider the status and function of an institution such as the university within this practice), that looks at the
full range of sites and spaces in which meaning is communicated (and the subject and social are produced), that explores with
students the kinds of questions we've been raising in our own

discussion, and finally, that might take as its subject post-politics, austerity capitalism and the corporatization of the university (and so what it can to provide students with the concepts to understand these developments)?

On the other hand I can't help but worry that the embrace of cultural studies within universities—to the limited degree that this has happened—is evidence of some of the pressures faced by the contemporary university. Raymond Williams famously identified three elements of culture: dominant, residual and emergent. The arts and humanities within universities reflect the dominant values of society, though they are also importantly residual insofar as their configuration represents a different social formation than that of the present. Within the relative autonomy that exists for many of those operating within universities, should we not instead try to occupy the position of the emergent? At their very best, cultural studies are driven by the imperative to do just this.

MJL: I agree with you about the need to affirm the mediating role of institutions. Universities definitely contribute to the creation of social values and creative industry advocates typically ignore this educational contribution that the welfare state makes to the general economy. If I could ask you one last question, I would be interested in knowing what kinds of policy issues are foremost in your mind at this moment in both the national situation and in terms of globalization. With the re-election of the Harper Conservatives and the arrival of Sun News, many in the various arts sectors in Canada are expecting the state to push culture further in the direction of a commercial and free market orientation—the kind of policy offensive that we've seen recently with the memorandum put out by the Dutch State Secretary for Culture. George Yúdice makes the observation that in the context of globalization, and even if the neoliberal state maintains public funding for culture, "culture-as-resource" acts as an expedient, both in terms of economic stimulus and with regard to the management of social conflicts (2003). The exemption of culture from free trade deals like NAFTA has proven to be something of a myth, however, and this is borne out in some respects as culture wars replace notions of national culture, or dovetail with it. Yúdice argues that trade liberalization has made culture more of a protagonist than it ever was. Beyond what you've already said about cosmopolitanism and universal access, what do you think of this special place of culture in the midst of global class polarization and proletarianization? Are the free traders correct? Is culture the ultimate commodity? I ask you this in part because our first meeting was in Montreal in March 2011 on the occasion of a lecture you gave at the Sauvé Scholars Foundation that was provocatively titled "Why We Don't Need Creativity."

IS: Let me talk first about why I don't think we need creativity. The 'we' is not just the left, or cultural producers, but *everyone*. And it isn't that we don't need novelty, or innovation, or change, or radical insights or interventions: it's creativity specifically that I think we don't need. I argue that creativity has become not just an empty honorific (the kind of thing that one says in praise of one's children) but also a dangerous one. It is a concept that is imagined as lying at the heart of artistic and cultural activity. Over the course of the twentieth-century, but with special force during the past two decades of globalization discourse, creativity has also come to be associated with any and all kinds of innovation in the business community. What I find significant about (for instance) Richard Florida's *The Rise of the Creative Class* (2002) is the manner in which he tries to connect the (supposed) autonomy of artists and cultural workers to the work of those involved in the high tech industry. Florida's argument is that more and more workers are becoming freer and freer (and also generating more money) because they are engaged in creative work in a manner that is similar to artists. In his eyes, artists have the maximum creativity, spending their days engaged in self-expression and self-definition. We're lucky then to live at a moment when *all* work becomes akin to being an artist, as we can thus express our creativity at work as well as at play.

What Florida and other champions of creativity overlook is, first, that many artists and cultural workers continue to receive far from living wages, and second, that those who are being creative in the tech industries are also receiving salaries that are less than they otherwise might. The (supposed) joys of being able to be creative seem to blind these workers to the fact that their employers are still making a surplus off of their labor. But even beyond this, I can't help but be suspicious of the very idea of creativity. It seems to do little real analytic work in comparison to its ideological function, which can range from expressions of pleasure or approval, to covering up the exploitation and the extraction of surplus through the narrative that we are all artists now, and so have reached whatever self-fulfillment we might expect from society. Creativity is far from a coherent concept, though we often enough take it to be so. In my reading of Florida's work, creativity has multiple, often contradictory definitions. It is at times an innate quality of the human everyone possesses; at other times, this quality is shared unequally, such that only some will ever be creative (and this is determined genetically); sometimes it is a cultural characteristic (some cultures being more creative than others); other times it is associated with certain kinds of work; frequently it is tied simply to innovation, and even more specifically, to innovations in technology.

For artists and cultural producers, the sudden importance of creative labor—and associated concepts, such as creative cities —might make it seem as if it their own work has finally assumed the social importance they always imagined for it. To whatever degree, in an effort to develop the immaterial and affective aspects of their economies in the new century, cities, regions and countries around the world have created programs to support and encourage culture. Instead of being a drain on economies, the arts and culture sector is now seen as a having a positive fiscal impact on the economy. So one might think: even if creativity is a specious concept, what could be wrong with taking advantage of creative discourses that help generate more money for museums, increase grants for artists, expand government sponsorship of festivals, and so on?

I don't see it this way. The use of the concept of creativity to render non-cultural activities as having the same freedom as artists' work functions to transform a romantic fiction of the latter into a way of affirming the permanence of labor under capitalism—which now becomes okay because it is creative, and so unalienated, too! It also undermines the relative autonomy of arts and culture—an autonomy (however questionable, however problematic at a theoretical level) that enabled and supported a critical vantage point on the social and political. Yúdice writes that "the role of culture has expanded in an unprecedented way into the political and economic at the same time that conventional notions of culture largely have been emptied out" (9). If culture has become a protagonist, it is only through an emptying out of any critical notion of the arts and culture. It may well be that culture is the ultimate commodity. The profit margins on cultural goods can be huge, and it seems to be as necessary to our daily lives as food and water. But this of course is a further problem of our moment as opposed to anything like a solution—a collapse of art and life that is perverse in ways well beyond the trauma of the rise of mass culture that concerned Peter Bürger in his meditations on the fate of the avant garde. And though one element of capital might champion creative culture and creative cities, I suspect that even so it is funding for arts and culture that will be most deeply impacted by austerity measures around the globe. As the Dutch example you point to makes evident, when money is in short supply, whether due to a lack of taxes coming in (in the case of states) or a drop in consumer spending, there is a quick turn to 'vulgar' analyses of what is most socially significant or important. Culture and the arts usually don't cut it—and I should add, this vulgar analysis doesn't always need fiscal shortfalls to animate states or cause companies to reduce their support.

We're in an interregnum. We continue to operate with older ideas of the critical capacities of art and culture. We've challenged from multiple perspectives some of the problems and limits of a critical autonomy that comes only through a separation from life. Yet given the examples of an art integrated with life, whether this is Bourriaud's aesthetics or the world of immaterial labor named in Florida's use of creativity, we can't help but want to return to an older configuration of the politics of the aesthetics, unless we decide to abandon the equation of art and politics entirely. This is something that, for instance, Gerald Raunig seems to do in *Art and Revolution*, where he renarrates the avant garde as a series of "transitions, overlaps and concatenations of art and revolution [that] become possible for a limited time, but without synthesis and identification" (17-18). But to say we're in an interregnum is far from saying that things are hopeless, or that art is compromised and can generate no political insight or action.

Surveying the landscape of contemporary art, Rasmussen offers the following account of where aesthetics stands in relation to politics at the present time:

> traditional forms of intellectual and aesthetic opposition no longer seem to be at all available. Visual images as well as words and music appear to lack their former alienating effect and are rarely antagonistic towards the prevailing order. Wherever we direct our gaze, it is the complicity of the art institution with the established power that is most conspicuous. The speculation economy of neoliberal capitalism pumped huge sums of money into the art market after 1989, with the result that art today is closely tied to the transnational circulation of capital. At the same time national governments, provinces and cities use art as a marketing instrument in the febrile competition for manpower, investments and tourists. These developments towards an ever-closer link between art and capital, and between art and the ruling order, are undoubtedly the predominant tendency when it comes to contemporary art. (199)

This passage can be read as listing a series of failures—as the ever-greater deterioration of the critical capacities of art and culture. But it can also be read as a blunt, non-moralizing description of where we are, whether we like it or not; that is, as an outline of the challenging circumstances in which we find ourselves. Is it a complete list? No. However, by not naming those critical capacities and possibilities that do exist it is pessimistic and one-sided in the extreme. And there is a developmental narrative suggested that is often present when we paint pictures of where we find ourselves, one that suggests that an open door that once existed is not only being closed but written out of the picture. Better instead to understand that every moment has its crises and problems. Our challenge as scholars is to understand these so that we might do our part in making sure that what appears on the other side of the interregnum is a reality we would want to live in rather than merely endure.

References

Agamben, Giorgio. *The Coming Community*, trans. Michael Hardt (Minneapolis: University of Minnesota Press, [1990] 1993).

Archibugi, Daniele. "Cosmopolitical Democracy." In Daniele Archibugi, ed. *Debating Cosmopolitics* (New York: Verso, 2003) 1-15.

Brennan, Timothy. "Cosmopolitanism and Internationalism." In Daniele Archibugi, ed. *Debating Cosmopolitics* (New York: Verso, 2003) 40-50.

Cazdyn, Eric and Imre Szeman. *After Globalization* (Oxford: Wiley-Blackwell, 2011).

Florida, Richard. *The Rise of the Creative Class* (New York: Basic Books, 2002).

Foster, Hal. "Chat Rooms." In Claire Bishop, ed. *Participation* (Cambridge, MA: The MIT Press, 2006) 190-195.

---. "Towards a Grammar of Emergency." *New Left Review* 68 (2011) 105-118.

Harvey, David. "Feral Capitalism Hits The Streets." *The Bullet* (August 12, 2011). Web.

Jameson, Fredric. "Transformations of the Image in Postmodernity." *The Cultural Turn: Selected Writings on the Postmodern, 1983-1998* (New York: Verso, 1998) 93-135.

Kant, Immanuel. "Perpetual Peace: A Philosophical Sketch." *An Answer to the Question: What is Enlightenment?*, trans. H.B. Nisbet (New York: Penguin Books, 2009).

The Power of Community: How Cuba Survived Peak Oil. Directed by Faith Morgan. USA, 2006.

Rancière, Jacques. *The Politics of Aesthetics*, trans. Gabriel Rockhill (London: Continuum, 2004).

Rasmussen, Mikkel Bolt. "Scattered (Western Marxist-Style) Remarks about Contemporary Art, Its Contradictions and Difficulties." *Third Text* 25:2 (2011) 199-210.

Raunig, Gerald. *Art and Revolution: Transversal Activism in the Long Twentieth Century*, trans. Aileen Derieg (Los Angeles: Semiotext(e), 2007).

Szeman, Imre. "Imagining the Future: Globalization, Postmodernism and Criticism." *Frame: Tijdschrift voor Literatuurwetenschap* (Netherlands) 19:2 (2006) 16-30; http://individual.utoronto.ca/nishashah/Drafts/Szeman.pdf

Szeman, Imre, "Marxist Literary Criticism, Then and Now," *Mediations* 24:2 (Spring 2009); http://www.mediationsjournal.org/articles/marxist-literary-criticism-then-and-now

Szeman, Imre. "Neoliberals Dressed in Black; or, the Traffic in Creativity." *English Studies in Canada* 36:1 (2010) 15-38.

Wright, Erik Olin. *Envisioning Real Utopias* (New York: Verso, 2010).

Yúdice, George. *The Expediency of Culture: Uses of Culture in the Global Era* (Durham: Duke University Press, 2003).

[insurgencies]

Everyone is a Terrorist Now: Marginalizing Protest in the U.S.

IVAN GREENBERG[1]

Political policing (or state "high policing") usually is defined as activity which is directed, through surveillance and counterinsurgency, to control particular groups and communities. It is not deviant behavior but a core function of government to protect a political regime. In the U.S. context, the practice has deep historical roots and almost always is done secretly because it undermines the intention of the First Amendment, which protects free speech and assembly. Until the mid-1970s, most American political policing was directed against actors identified as "subversive." Afterwards, the category of "terrorism" became the legal basis for most domestic security investigations.[2] While this change from subversion to terrorism was intended to reduce government spying, one effect has been stigma and marginalization: the labeling of protest as terrorism undermines the legitimacy of a wide range of political expression. In

---

[1] Ivan Greenberg is the author of two books on surveillance, civil liberties, and surveillance in the U.S. The most recent is *Surveillance in America: Critical Analysis of the FBI, 1920 to the Present* (Lexington Books, 2012). He earned a PhD from the CUNY Graduate Center.

[2] Ivan Greenberg, *The Dangers of Dissent: The FBI and Civil Liberties Since 1965* (Lanham, MD: Lexington Books, 2010); Athan G. Theoharis, "Political Policing in the United States: The Evolution of the FBI, 1917-1956," in Mark Mazower, ed., *The Policing of Politics in the Twentieth Century: Historical Perspectives* (Oxford: Berghahn Books, 1997), 191-212.

the era of the "war on terror" against radical Islam, the concept of what constitutes terrorist activity is thoroughly confused. The American state deliberately makes little distinction between fighting violent terrorism with overseas roots and fighting peaceful, legal, domestic political activity. In the FBI's view, terrorists are found everywhere there is disagreement and conflict in society. Indeed, the very act of criticizing the government outside of a protest movement can result in being labeled a terrorist. Even though American radicals rarely commit crimes, the FBI claims they pose a major challenge to peaceful order in society. The terrorist label so broadly has been misapplied that it has lost most significance and meaning.

The level of political violence in the U.S. is very low regardless of whether it originates overseas or at home. Yet, despite the absence of violent acts, the U.S. government touts the threat as a top danger to the nation. It needs terrorists to exist and wants America to face a terrorist threat. If there is no real threat, they must fabricate one. This fabrication allows the FBI to surveil and attack oppositional political formations. Since there are so few real terrorists, the government has built up a phony threat, a ghost of a menace, a "scare" that does not have much grounding in reality. It serves conservative political interests.

WHAT IS TERRORISM?

In its effort to contain dissent, the American government benefits that definitions of terrorism vary widely. In both academic and government discourse, a consensus does not exist about what terrorism involves, which has allowed powerful interests to distort terrorism debates. In academic discourse, Lisa Stampnitzky notes, "One of the most oft-noted difficulties has been the inability of researchers to establish a suitable definition of the concept of 'terrorism' itself, with the result that practically every book, essay, and article on the topic has been compelled to take on this so- called 'problem of definition.'"[3]   Meanwhile, in governmental politics the United Nations, for example, cannot agree on a definition.   Since 9/11, the U.N. has

---

[3] Lisa Stampnitzky, "Disciplining an Unruly Field: Terrorism Experts and Theories of Scientific/Intellectual Problems," *Qualitative Sociology*, 34 (March 2011): 3.

proved unable to gain consensus on any comprehensive statement or action on the issue. Since no universally accepted definition exists within the international community, anti-terror measures vary widely by nation. Indeed, in the decade after 9/11 more than 140 nations passed new anti-terrorism laws. In many cases, the new legislation justified increased repression toward domestic populations.

Human Rights Watch points to the "dangerous expansion of powers to detain and prosecute people, including peaceful political opponents...the tendency of these laws to cover a wide range of conduct far beyond what is generally understood as terrorist. More often than not, the laws define terrorism using broad and open-ended language." The threat to domestic dissent is real. "In dozens of countries, acts of political dissent that result in property damage, such as demonstrations, may be prosecuted as terrorism where the element of terrorist intent is broadly defined (for example, to 'disrupt the public order' or 'endanger public safety')." More than 50 of the new counter-terror laws in the U.S. place new restrictions on speech by criminalizing expression that encourages terrorism absent any charge of incitement to violence, and more than 120 laws vastly expand police surveillance and detention powers. Moreover, governments in several nations "redefined longstanding armed conflicts as part of the 'global war on terror' for internal political purposes or to gain international support." For example, Russia views the conflict in Chechnya as a struggle against international terrorists, not as a separatist conflict.[4]

In considering the U.S. conflation of dissent with terrorism, it is useful to consult the new field of Critical Terrorism Studies (CTS). CTS adopts the view that existing counter-terror policies often serve the interests of hegemonic power structures to maintain the status quo. Terrorism is a social construction and different groups and forces in society conceptualize it differently. CTS casts a critical eye on state power both as a perpetrator of political violence and for manufacturing ideas contrary to

---

[4] Human Rights Watch, "In the Name of Security: Counterterrorism Laws Worldwide since September 11," June 29, 2012, 4, 6, 21-22, 41, 51, www.hrw.org/reports/2012/06/29/name-security. See also Kent Roach, *The 9/11 Effect: Comparative Counter-Terrorism* (New York: Cambridge University Press, 2011).

emancipatory objectives. In the debut issue of *Critical Studies on Terrorism* in 2008, the editors outlined a series of topics that had received scant attention, including: the role of state terrorism; the effects of the war on terror on poor peoples; the cultural construction of terrorism; and the "ideographic qualities" of the terrorism label.[5]

PROTEST AS TERRORISM

A major reason the FBI calls nonviolent protestors terrorists is related to official FBI Guidelines for investigation developed by the U.S. Department of Justice. According to these Guidelines, the FBI is instructed to respect the First Amendment and civil liberties. The Bureau is forbidden to investigate the politics of Americans unless they can be linked to advocacy of violence or efforts to organize violent acts. "These Guidelines do not authorize investigating or collecting or maintaining information on United States persons solely for the purpose of monitoring activities protected by the First Amendment or the lawful exercise of other rights secured by the Constitution or laws of the United States."[6]

A fuller statement of the FBI's alleged respect for legal and Constitutional rights is contained in a Bureau document distributed to its personnel: the *Domestic Investigations and Operations Guide* (DIOG). Strong civil liberty protections are outlined, as if an attorney from the American Civil Liberties Union (ACLU) had written these sections. Nearly 20 pages of DIOG are devoted to "Privacy and Civil Liberties, and Least Intrusive Methods." The document states:

> Protecting the public includes protecting their rights and liberties. FBI investigative activity is premised upon the fundamental duty of government to protect the public, which must be performed with

---

[5] Marie Breen Smyth, Jeroen Gunning, Richard Jackson, George Kassimeris, and Piers Robinson, "Critical Terrorism Studies –An introduction," *Critical Studies on Terrorism*, 1 (April 2008): 3. See also Richard Jackson, Marie Breen Smyth, and Jeroen Gunning, eds., *Critical Terrorism Studies: A New Research Agenda* (New York: Routledge, 2009).

[6] U.S. Department of Justice, "The Attorney General's Guidelines for Domestic FBI Operations," 2008, 13, http://www.justice.gov/ag/readingroom/guidelines.pdf (accessed Aug. 19, 2012)

care to protect individual rights and to ensure that investigations are confined to matters of legitimate government interest...

Race, ethnicity, religion, or national origin alone can never constitute the sole basis for initiating investigative activity...

Employ the least intrusive means that do not otherwise compromise FBI operations. Assuming a lawful intelligence or evidence collection objective, an authorized purpose, strongly consider the method (technique) employed to achieve that objective that is the least intrusive available (particularly if there is the potential to interfere with protected speech and association, damage someone's reputation, intrude on privacy, or interfere with the sovereignty of foreign governments) while still being operationally sound and effective.[7]

A second important FBI document, the "FBI Agents Legal Handbook," outlines restrictions on uses of informers. This is not a minor matter since informers function as a key undercover spying tool. The FBI cannot direct these "human assets" to act in ways that are forbidden for other FBI personnel. The Handbook states:

Although informers are private individuals in the sense that they are not commissioned representatives of the government, they are considered agents of the government when performing informant-related tasks....As such, they are subject to the same legal restrictions that govern the conduct of Special Agents. It follows that if the informant's contemplated action would be illegal or unconstitutional if performed by a Special Agent, it is also impermissible if performed by the informant.[8]

FBI public documents echo these private ones. In the document, "Our Responsibility to Protect Civil Liberties," the FBI states:

The FBI is committed to carrying out its mission in accordance with the protections provided by the Constitution. FBI agents are trained to understand and appreciate that the responsibility to respect and protect the law is the basis for their authority to enforce it. The FBI

---

[7] Federal Bureau of Investigation, "FBI Domestic Investigations and Operations Guide (DOIG) 2011," October 15, 2011, 69, www.vault.fbi.gov (accessed Aug. 19, 2012).

[8] Federal Bureau of Investigation, "FBI Agents Legal Handbook," Aug. 20, 2003, 112, http://fbiexpert.com/FBI_Manuals/Legal_Handbook_for_Special_Agents/FBI_Agents_Legal_Handbook.pdf

puts a premium on thoroughly training our special agents about their responsibility to respect the rights and dignity of individuals.[9]

An article titled "Domestic Terrorism," which is posted on the FBI website, asserts:

> Hate and anger are not crimes; neither are hard-line and poisonous ideologies. It's only when actions by groups or individuals cross the line into threats, the actual use of force or violence, or other law-breaking activities that we can investigate.[10]

Thus, the limitations on FBI spying seem significant. But in practice these Guidelines, Handbooks, and public pronouncements carry little weight. The FBI subverts them by calling everyone terrorists and by claiming the threat is severe or imminent. It is official dishonesty in secret documents that few outside the FBI can access. Unaccountability is integral to the mislabeling of political activity.

As part of the "criminalization of dissent," associating speech and writing, as well as peaceful social action, with terrorism functions to discredit subjects. The state smears political opponents as dangerous and disloyal in order to marginalize them. Although subjects of FBI terrorism investigation often are not arrested, the investigations allow the government to collect intelligence to be used to undermine social movements based, for example, on anti-war, anti-capitalist, or anti-globalization politics.

The USA Patriot Act (2001) codified a loose definition of terrorism in federal law. Section 802 created the federal crime of "domestic terrorism" to cover "acts dangerous to human life that are in violation of the criminal laws of the United States or of any State." A terrorist act consisted of any effort "to intimidate or coerce a civilian population" or "to influence the policy of government by intimidation or coercion." The precise meaning of intimidation and coercion remains unclear. The FBI has viewed peaceful civil disobedience as terrorism.[11]

---

[9] Federal Bureau of Investigation, "Our Responsibility to Protect Civil Liberties," http://www.fbi.gov/about-us/intelligence/liberties (accessed Aug. 19, 2012).

[10] Federal Bureau of Investigation, "Domestic Terrorism," Sept. 9, 2009, http://www.fbi.gov/news/stories/2009/september/domterror_090709.

Despite the Patriot Act, disagreement exists within the government about what constitutes terrorist behavior. In 2010, the Office of the Inspector General at the Justice Department reviewed FBI surveillance of five domestic political advocacy groups and found the FBI misapplied the terrorism classification. The Bureau "relied upon potential crimes that may not commonly be considered as 'terrorism' (such as trespassing or vandalism) and that alternatively have been classified differently, such as under the classification for crimes on government reservations."[12]

Moreover, the vast majority of criminal charges brought by the FBI for terrorism do not hold up in court. In 2008, government prosecutors declined to bring charges against 73 percent of the criminal cases referred to them for terrorism, up from 61 percent in 2005. Syracuse University's TRAC research group found: "Federal agencies can't seem to agree on who is a terrorist and who is not. The failure has potentially serious implications, weakening efforts to use the criminal law to combat terrorism and at the same time undermining civil liberties."[13] This uneven approach points to a pattern of abuse. Falsely charging a person with terrorism, even if prosecution fails, is a form of state harassment. It also is one way the FBI manipulates public opinion to build up the gravity of the threat. Arrests make headlines and the public is led to believe a grave danger exists. By contrast, the dismissal of charges rarely makes headlines; and the pattern of overcharging rarely is discussed in popular media discourse.

---

[11] Jules Boykoff, *Beyond Bullets: The Suppression of Dissent in the United States* (Oakland, CA: AK Press, 2007), 293–95; Nancy Chang, *Silencing Political Dissent: How Post-September 11 Anti-terrorism Measures Threaten Our Civil Liberties* (New York: Seven Stories Press, 2002), 112.

[12] The five groups were: Thomas Merton Center; Society of Friends (Quakers); Greenpeace USA; People for the Ethical Treatment of Animals (PETA); and the Catholic Worker. Office of Inspector General, U. S. Department of Justice, "A Review of the FBI's Investigations of Certain Domestic Advocacy Groups," September 2010, 1-2, 188.

[13] Transactional Records Access Clearinghouse (TRAC), "Who is a Terrorist? Government Failure to Define Terrorism Undermines Enforcement Puts Civil Liberties at Risk," Sept. 28, 2009, 1-2, http://trac.syr.edu/tracreports/terrorism/215/.

Under the banner of fighting terrorism, U.S. intelligence agencies monitor popular websites, blogs, and message boards unrelated to specific groups and individuals. The U.S. Department of Homeland Security (DHS) has taken the lead in a program called "Social Networking/Media Capability." DHS tracked dozens of popular sites to identify criticism of U.S. policies. They call it "situational awareness": popular opinion about news events that "reflect adversely" on the U.S. government. As one prominent example, DHS conducted mass monitoring of Facebook to "capture public reaction" regarding the possible relocation of Guantanamo terror detainees to a prison in Michigan. DHS also monitored the comments section to articles in the *New York Times*, *Los Angeles Times*, and the *HuffingtonPost* looking to identify criticism of the intelligence community. Other websites under surveillance include:

Twitter	Hulu	My Space
YouTube	Flickr	Wikileaks
Drudge Report	ABC News	Wired
Cryptome	Jihad Watch	Informed Comment[14]

DHS employs analytical computer software in its monitoring, which relies on hundreds of key words and search terms to detect controversial political expression. The Electronic Privacy Information Center (EPIC) reports that the list includes "vast amounts of First Amendment protected speech that is entirely unrelated to the Department of Homeland Security mission to protect the public against terrorism and disasters."[15] Fifty-six words or terms are listed under the category of "domestic security."[16] (See Tables 1-3, below.) When these terms appear in a

---

[14] "Homeland Security Watches Twitter, Social Media," *Reuters*, Jan. 11, 2012; Stone, Andrea. "DHS Monitoring of Social Media Under Scrutiny by Lawmakers," in *HuffingtonPost*, Feb. 16, 2012, http://www.huffingtonpost.com/2012/02/16/ dhs-monitoring-of-social-media_n_1282494.html ; "DHS Monitoring of Social Media Concerns Civil Liberties Advocates," *Washington Post*, Jan. 13, 2012.

[15] "Homeland Security Manual Lists Government Key Words for Monitoring Social Media, News," *HuffingtonPost*, Feb. 24, 2012, http://www.huffingtonpost.com/2012/02/24/homeland-security-manual_n_1299908.html.

[16] "Dept. of Homeland Security Forced to Release List of Keywords Used to Monitor Social Networking Sites," *Forbes* May 26, 2012, http://www.forbes.com/sites/reuvencohen/2012/05/26/department-of-

domestic communication, the whole message or article may be flagged for further inspection.

Most political intelligence gathered by DHS is made available to the FBI. The same sharing of information characterizes the Counter-Terrorism Unit of the Federal Bureau of Prisons.

TABLE 1: DOMESTIC SECURITY KEYWORDS

Assassination	Emergency management	Gangs
Attack	Emergency response	National security
Domestic security	First responder	State of emergency
Drill	Homeland security	Security
Exercise	Maritime domain awareness (MDA)	Breach
Cops	National Preparedness initiative	Threat
Law enforcement	Militia	Standoff
Authorities	Shooting	SWAT
Disaster assistance	Shots fired	Screening
Disaster management	Evacuation	Bomb (squad or threat)
DNDO (Domestic Nuclear Detection Office)	Deaths	Crash
Mitigation	Hostage	Looting
Prevention	Explosion (explosive)	Riot

homeland-security-forced-to-release-list-of-keywords-used-to-monitor-social-networking-sites/.

TABLE 1 (...CONT'D): DOMESTIC SECURITY KEYWORDS

Response	Police	Pipe Bomb
Dirty Bomb	Organized crime	Incident
Facility		

TABLE 2: HAZMAT & NUCLEAR KEYWORDS

Hazmat	Leak	Gas
Nuclear	Biological infection (or event)	Spillover
Chemical spill	Chemical	Anthrax
Suspicious package/device	Chemical burn	Blister agent
Toxic	Biological	Chemical agent
National laboratory	Epidemic	Exposure
Nuclear facility	Hazardous	Burn
Cloud	Hazardous material incident	Ricin
Plume	Industrial spill	Sarin
Radiation	Infection	North Korea
Radioactive	Powder (white)	

TABLE 3: HEALTH CONCERN + H1N1 KEYWORDS

Outbreak	Salmonella	Agriculture
Contamination	Small Pox	Listeria
Exposure	Plague	Symptoms
Virus	Human to human	Mutation
Evacuation	Human to animal	Resistant
Bacteria	Influenza	Antiviral
Recall	Center for Disease Control (CDC)	Wave
Ebola	Drug Administration (FDA)	Pandemic
Food Poisoning	Public Health	Infection
Foot and Mouth (FMD)	Toxic	Water/air borne
H5N1	AgroTerror	Swine
Avian Flu	Tuberculosis (TB)	Pork

Author Will Potter obtained government documents revealing this Unit maintains files about journalists whose writings, interviews, and lectures are critical of government repression. Potter found multiple references to his own book, *Green is the New Red*, about government attacks on the environmental and animal rights movement. Several of Potter's public lectures also were monitored. In one lecture, he

> spoke about how 'terrorists' have become the new enemy of the hour and a rhetorical tool to excuse all manner of harassment, intimidation, and surveillance…What does it say about our govern-

ment and our culture's understanding of 'terrorism threats' that
these dossiers included articles, speeches, and books?[17]

The state strategy of calling everyone a terrorist is underappre-
ciated in U.S popular consciousness. On the one hand, there
may be general timidity to directly challenge the dominant
ideas and practices of the intelligence community, fearful that
such criticism might prompt state countermeasures. The FBI,
for example, has a long history of tracking its critics. On the
other hand, it is difficult for dissidents to advance ideas on this
subject because the mainstream media rarely allows such questioning of the intelligence community.

In 2012, a major U.S. Senate report found significant
ineffectiveness in domestic anti-terror efforts related to official
"fusion centers." The DHS runs about 70 such centers across
the nation to consolidate and analyze regional political
intelligence. While the Congressional report referred to
"wasteful" spending and "irrelevant" and "useless" intelligence
reporting, it did not acknowledge political policing as a
function of government.[18] Yet, there is little doubt protest
movements in America continue.to be subject to state scrutiny.
Recent revelations about government spying on the Occupy
movement in more than 15 cities demonstrates, once again, that
DHS and the FBI labeled homegrown protestors as terrorists.
FBI memos refer to "domestic terrorism" and note local Joint
Terrorism Task Forces helped in "counterterrorism
preparedness" and "WMD [Weapons of Mass Destruction]
preparedness." In Los Angeles, the social control function
explicitly was articulated after a legal, nonviolent Occupy
protest in the subway system. The government worried about
Occupy alliances with the homeless.

---

[17] Will Potter, "Counter-Terrorism Unit Keeps Files on Journalists, Reports
that My Book is 'Compelling and Well Written,'" July 26, 2012,
http://www.greenisthenewred.com/blog/counter-terrorism-unit-keeps-files-on-
journalists/6247/.

[18] "DHS 'Fusion Centers' Portrayed as Pools of Ineptitude, Civil Liberties
Intrusions," *Washington Post*, Oct. 2, 2012; U.S. Senate Homeland Security
and Governmental Affairs Committee, "Investigative Report Criticizes
Counterterrorism Reporting, Waste at State and Local Intelligence Fusion
Centers," Oct. 3, 2012, http://www.hsgac.senate.gov/subcommittees/
investigations/media/ investigative-report-criticizes-counterterrorism-
reporting-waste-at-state-and-local-intelligence-fusion-centers

> [Text redacted] stated that transit-related crime in Los Angeles County has gone up recently...[Text redacted] blames the rising crime rate on mostly economic factors. In tough economic times, many shelters and care facilities for mentally ill individuals and drug users either close or have to turn people away. The aforementioned people account for a large percentage of the transit crime in the County of Los Angeles...
>
> On 10-19-2011 a peaceful protest by the 'Occupy Wall Street' movement occurred on a Blue Line train. [Text redacted] stated the protesters had all purchased tickets and were all cooperative. [Text redacted] is concerned however about what may happen if the 'Occupy Wall Street' protesters mix with the more violent individuals upset about the alleged mistreatment of prisoners in the LASD jails.[19]

In retrospect, the eventual police crackdown on the Occupy movement seems predictable since authorities have come to view protest through a prism of terrorism. The prospect of widespread repression in America hangs large before the people.

□ ◊ □□ ◊ □□ ◊ □

---

[19] FBI Los Angeles [Text redacted] to Los Angeles, "Intelligence Briefings or [sic] Liaison Squad I-1, Mass Transit (Surface)," Oct. 10, 2011. Declassified government spy documents on the Occupy Wall Street movement have been posted online by the Partnership for Civil Justice Fund, http://www.justiceonline.org/commentary/fbi-files-ows.html.

PUNCHING OUT PRESS.ORG

"Without a strategy that stems from common political agreement, revolutionary organizations are bound to be an affair of reactivism against the continual manifestations of oppression and injustice and/or a cycle of fruitless actions to be repeated over and over again, with little analysis or understanding of the consequences."

- Furious Five Collective,
on Especifismo

free · open
design, distro & incubation
originals & reprints:

essays · opinion · history · herstory · art ·
tactical manuals · strategic analysis

on the web:
PunchingOutPress.org
on twitter:
@punchingout

The Color of Corporate Corrections: The Overrepresentation of People of Color in the For-Profit Corrections Industry[1]

CHRISTOPHER PETRELLA[2] AND JOSH BEGLEY[3]

While data collected and maintained by the Federal Bureau of Prisons (BOP) and state departments of corrections (DOC) have long demonstrated the prevalence of persistent racial disparities in incarceration[4], no comparative study until now has illuminated the racial composition of select state-contracted, private prisons around the country.[5]

---

[1] This research report was submitted to both *Prison Legal News* and *Radical Criminology*. It first appeared in *Prison Legal News* and can also be accessed at www.prisonlegalnews.org. An updated version of *The Color of Corporate Corrections* study will appear in the next issue of *Radical Criminology* (#3), based on new information received from FOIA requests. In it, Christopher Petrella extends the examination of racial disparities in public vs. private prisons to include a large sample of U.S. states—19 in total—that incarcerate 500 or more adult men in secure and confined facilities managed by for-profit firms.

[2] Christopher Petrella is a doctoral candidate in African American Studies at U.C. Berkeley. His dissertation is entitled *"Race, Markets, and the Rise of the Private Prison State."* Learn more at www.christopherfrancispetrella.net

[3] Josh Begley is a graduate student in Interactive Telecommunications at NYU. You can follow him on Twitter (@joshbegley) or learn more at joshbegley.com.

[4] http://bjs.ojp.usdoj.gov/content/pub/pdf/p10.pdf

[5] In order to avoid artificially inflating the over-incarceration of people of color in for-profit prisons we intentionally excluded data from federal detention facilities controlled by the U.S. Immigration and Customs Enforcement (ICE) and the U.S. Marshals Service (USMS), as well as detention facilities managed at the local level. For this same reason, we strategically excluded data for transfer centers, work release centers,

Our conclusions reflect a rigorous multi-level analysis of the latest U.S. Census demographic figures available through the Prison Policy Initiative's "Correctional Facility Locator 2010" cross referenced with "count sheets," inmate population directories available on state DOC websites, and statistical information procured through Freedom of Information Act (FOIA) requests filed with the California Department of Corrections and Rehabilitation (CDCR).[6] Datasets were accessed from August-October 2012 and analyzed in November 2012.

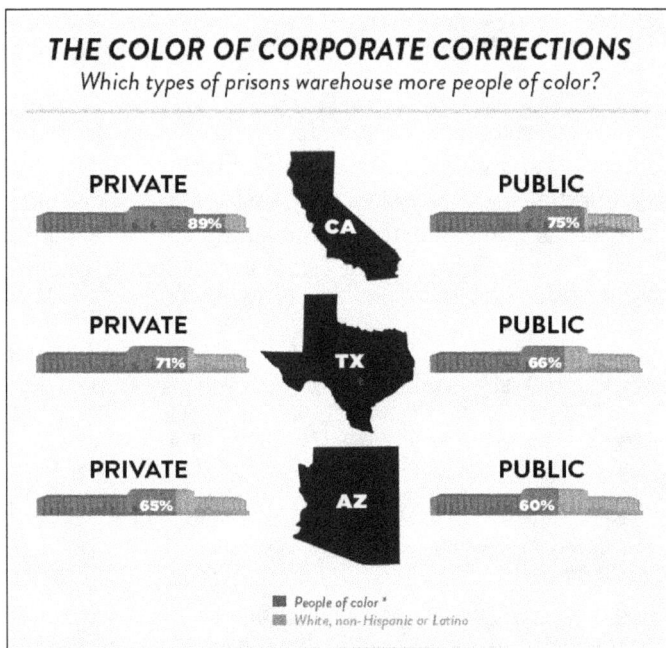

THE COLOR OF CORPORATE CORRECTIONS
Which types of prisons warehouse more people of color?

PRIVATE — CA — 89%   PUBLIC — CA — 75%

PRIVATE — TX — 71%   PUBLIC — TX — 66%

PRIVATE — AZ — 65%   PUBLIC — AZ — 60%

■ People of color *
■ White, non-Hispanic or Latino

We selected California, Texas, and Arizona for this study because they warehouse some of the largest numbers of inmates in private, for-profit prisons in the nation. Our sample size is large and reliable. Taken together, California, Texas, and Arizona account for over 1/3 of all prisoners housed in private facilities around the country. Although people of color[7] are al-

community correction facilities, special treatment centers, reception centers, and any facility with a population under 500 persons.

[6] http://www.prisonersofthecensus.org/locator2010/

[7] Although racial designations are always imprecise, elusive, and subject to revision, we appropriated U.S. Census Bureau racial categories for the

ready overrepresented in public prisons relative to their state and national population share[8], our research indicates that people of color are further overrepresented by roughly 12 percent in state-level correctional facilities operated by for-profit, private prison firms. This over-representation of people of color in for-profit, private corrections institutions should be a matter of deep public concern.

The private prison industry has arguably represented an experiment in racialization from its very inception. Corrections Corporation of America (CCA)—the nation's oldest and largest for-profit company which now controls 43 percent of the private corrections market—received its first contract in 1983 from the now defunct Immigration and Naturalization Services (INS), an agency primarily responsible for regulating the movement of bodies of color.[9] This trend continues today. According to stipulations articulated in a 2007 CDCR memorandum, the state of California prioritizes previously deported inmates and/or inmates with active *or* potential ICE (Immigration and Customs Enforcement) holds—a policy that disproportionately affects people of color—for involuntary transfers to out-of-state private facilities.[10]

Our sense is that applying privatization to the most vulnerable and politically marginalized racial groups allows state DOCs and the private prison industry to externalize costs without facing "legitimate" public backlash. The overrepresentation of bodies of color in private prison facilities suggests that communities of color are seen as unworthy of taxpayer supported *public investment.* That is, relative to for-profit correctional in-

purposes of this study to preserve nomenclatural, and therefore statistical, fidelity in our cross-referencing efforts. People of color here are defined as "Black, American Indian or Alaska Native, Asian, Native Hawaiian or Pacific Islander, and non-white Hispanic or Latino."

[8]People of color comprise 61 percent of California's population yet account for 75 percent of the state's public prison enrollment. In Texas, people of color comprise 55 percent of the state's population yet account for 66 percent of the public corrections population. And finally, people of color comprise 43 percent of Arizona's population yet account for 60 percent of the state's public prison share. http://quickfacts.census.gov/qfd/index.html

[9] http://ir.correctionscorp.com/ phoenix.zhtml?c=117983&p=irol-presentations

[10] https://www.aclunc.org/cases/closed_cases/asset_upload_file958_7840.pdf

stitutions, people of color are disproportionately siphoned away from public facilities, precisely the types of facilities that provide the most educational, pro-social, and rehabilitative programs.[11]

Instead, the overrepresentation of people of color in private, for-profit facilities—facilities with strikingly few rehabilitative programs relative to public corrections institutions—suggests that the containment of people of color, relative to "non-Hispanic, whites," functions primarily as a source of profit extraction. Whereas the primary objective of public corrections agencies is the promotion of public safety through rehabilitation, private prison firms are first accountable to their shareholders. Companies like CCA are legally obligated to increase shareholder value, an imperative that inherently compromises any deep commitment to rehabilitation, social re-entry, or recidivism reduction.

Our study also raises larger questions about the relationship between race and democracy. A substantial overrepresentation of people of color in facilities controlled by for-profit firms suggests that people of color are excluded from traditional national conceptions of "the commons" and therefore remain unable to participate fully in this nation's democratic experiment.

Though research pertaining to the racial composition of private prisons is still emerging, we're confident that our findings will generate substantive discussion on the relationship between race and prison privatization in the United States. Above all, we're hopeful that research like this—limited as it is—will inspire policies aimed at eliminating the for-profit corrections industry, an industry that disproportionately commoditizes people of color and subjects them to the whims of the highest bidder.

> The following pages of charts and graphs (Figures 1-6) were created by *Radical Criminology* in order to visually present the dataset submitted by Christopher Petrella & Josh Begley. These statistics break down the composition of the prison population in both public and private facilities of three US states'. [As stated, "[d]atasets were accessed from August-October 2012 and analyzed in November 2012."] Please look for our next issue for an updated, extended dataset, along with further research and analysis.   ***-Editor-***

---

[11] http://www.urban.org/projects/reentry-roundtable/upload/Crayton.pdf

Figure 1. Arizona
Public Facilities

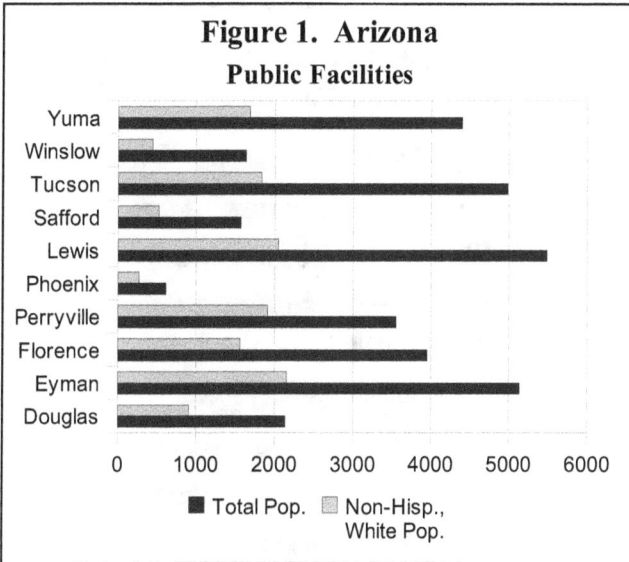

Yuma
Winslow
Tucson
Safford
Lewis
Phoenix
Perryville
Florence
Eyman
Douglas

0   1000   2000   3000   4000   5000   6000

■ Total Pop.   ▨ Non-Hisp., White Pop.

Figure 1.1. Arizona Public Facilities: Total Population

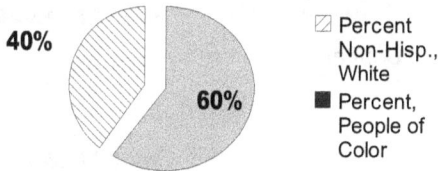

40%

60%

▨ Percent Non-Hisp., White

■ Percent, People of Color

Figure 2. Arizona
Private Facilities

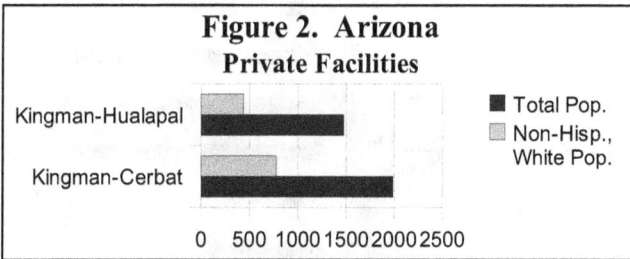

Kingman-Hualapal

Kingman-Cerbat

0   500 1000 1500 2000 2500

■ Total Pop.
▨ Non-Hisp., White Pop.

Figure 2.1. Arizona Private Facilities: Total Population

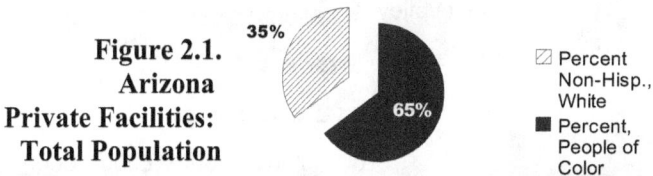

35%

65%

▨ Percent Non-Hisp., White

■ Percent, People of Color

Total Arizona Overrepresentation (Private Facilities, Persons-of-Color): **8%**

Figure 3. California
Public Facilities

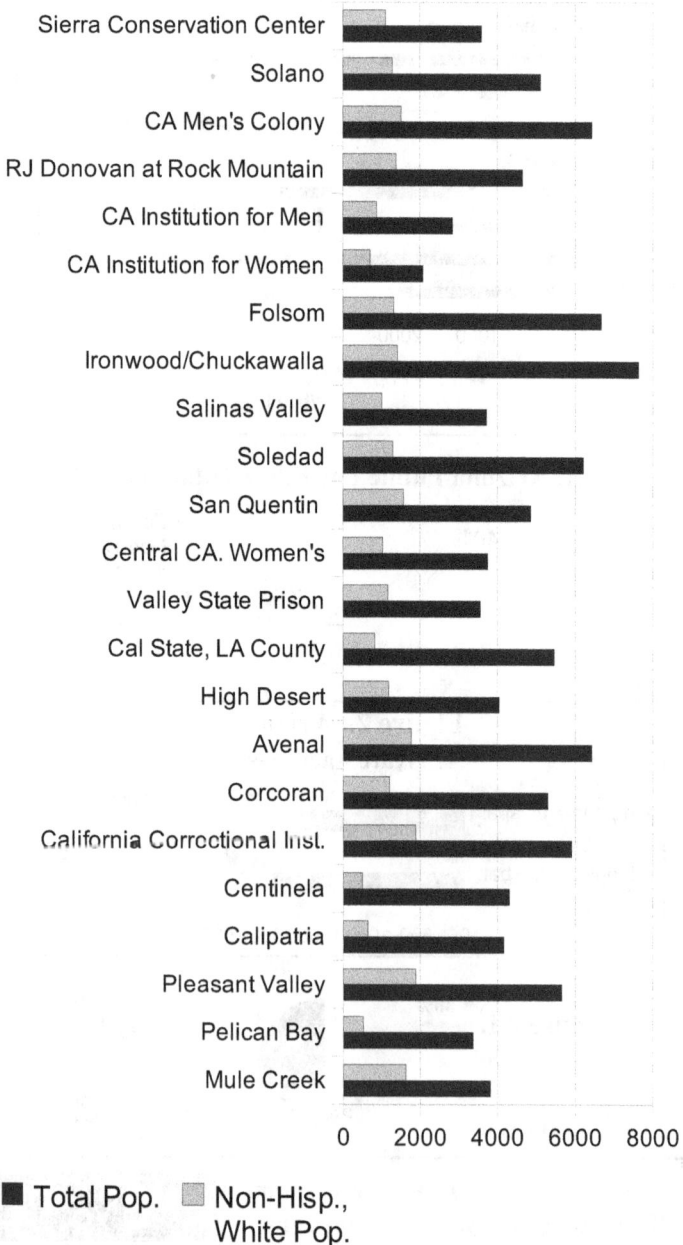

Sierra Conservation Center
Solano
CA Men's Colony
RJ Donovan at Rock Mountain
CA Institution for Men
CA Institution for Women
Folsom
Ironwood/Chuckawalla
Salinas Valley
Soledad
San Quentin
Central CA. Women's
Valley State Prison
Cal State, LA County
High Desert
Avenal
Corcoran
California Correctional Inst.
Centinela
Calipatria
Pleasant Valley
Pelican Bay
Mule Creek

0   2000   4000   6000   8000

■ Total Pop.   Non-Hisp.,
White Pop.

FIGURE 3.1. CALIFORNIA PUBLIC FACILITIES:
TOTAL POPULATION

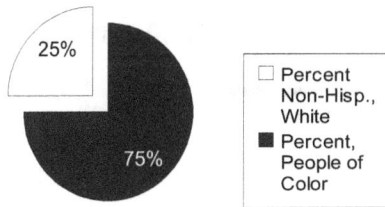

25%

75%

☐ Percent Non-Hisp., White
■ Percent, People of Color

FIGURE 4. CALIFORNIA PRIVATE FACILITIES

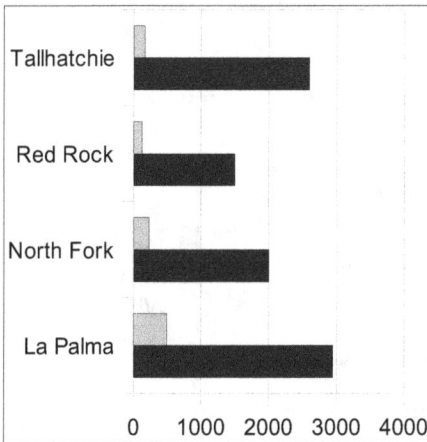

Tallhatchie

Red Rock

North Fork

La Palma

0   1000 2000 3000 4000

FIGURE 4.1. CALIFORNIA PRIVATE FACILITIES:
TOTAL POPULATION

▨ Percent Non-Hisp., White   ■ Percent, People of Color

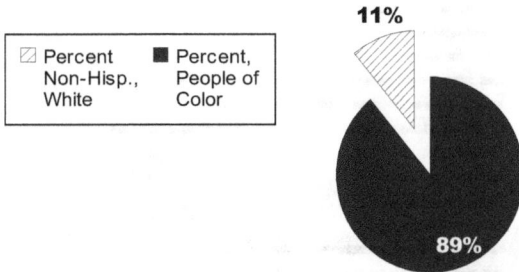

11%

89%

Total California Overrepresentation (Private Facilities, Persons-of-Color) as Percentage:	19%

Figure 5. Texas

Public Facilities

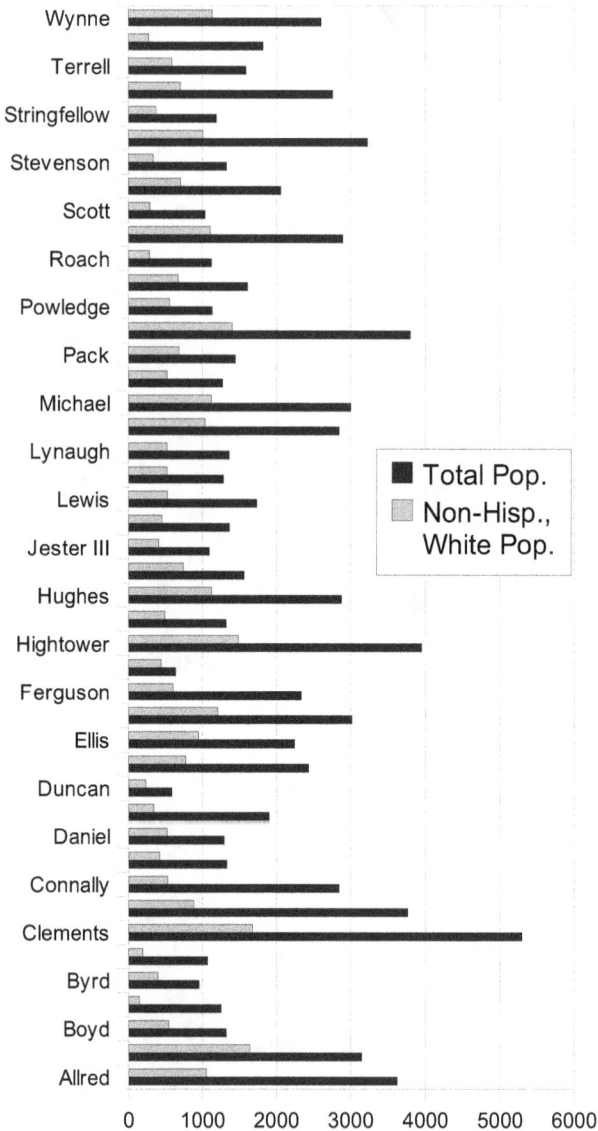

FIGURE 5.1 TEXAS PUBLIC FACILITIES: TOTAL POPULATION

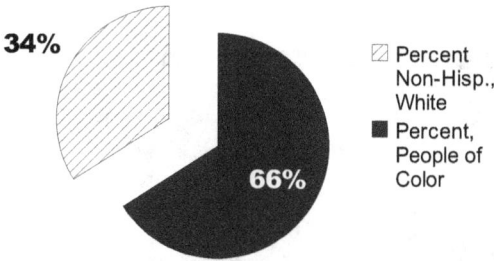

34%

66%

- ⊿ Percent Non-Hisp., White
- ■ Percent, People of Color

FIGURE 6. TEXAS PRIVATE FACILITIES

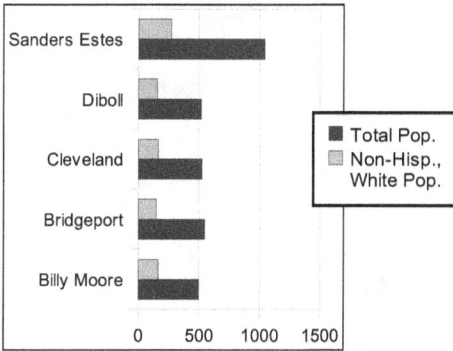

Sanders Estes
Diboll
Cleveland
Bridgeport
Billy Moore

- ■ Total Pop.
- ▨ Non-Hisp., White Pop.

0   500   1000   1500

FIGURE 6.1 TEXAS PRIVATE FACILITIES: TOTAL POPULATION

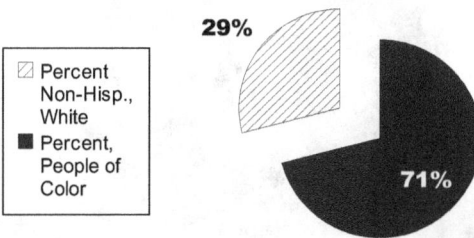

29%

71%

- ⊿ Percent Non-Hisp., White
- ■ Percent, People of Color

Total Texas **(Private Facilities, Persons-of-Color)** **Overrepresentation, as Percentage:**	**8%**
Total Over-representation in Private **Prisons (Arizona, California & Texas):**	**12%**

UPPING THE ANTI

...a journal of theory and action...

subscribe + submit
WWW.UPPINGTHEANTI.ORG

[book reviews]

The Criminal's Handbook: A Practical Guide to Surviving Arrest in Canada
Michael, C.W.
(London, ON: Insomniac Press, 2012. 288 pages.)

Reviewed by—Tom C. Allen,
Kwantlen Polytechnic University, July 2013

Most criminal justice books are written from the perspective of academics in ivory towers who have never had to deal with police officers who can legally lie during interrogations, 'dump truck' lawyers who take on far too many cases, or correctional officers who exaggerate reasons to lock down institutions so they can collect overtime. C.W. Michael's, *The Criminal's Handbook,* is an excellent resource not just for anyone who is in conflict with the law but for anyone interested in learning about the Canadian criminal justice system from the perspective of someone who has been there.

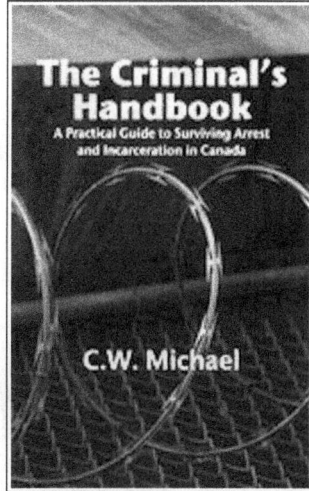

'Truth' needs to be understood not just from the top but also from the ground. I showed this book to a couple of colleagues[1],

---

[1] I am currently a criminology faculty at a Canadian university.

both with psychological backgrounds, and they summarily dismissed the text with 'It's anecdotal' and 'Where are the random samples?' This saddens me and leaves me to question the production of 'truth claims' in the university classroom. As the author states,

> A popular publication used by criminologists, students, and puppeteers of criminology is the *Canadian Journal of Criminology and Criminal Justice,* a journal which is partly funded by CSC [Correctional Services Canada]. One should wonder if that is much different from a tobacco corporation keeping a doctor on the payroll to issue reports on the health effects of smoking (86).

To understand the street we must hear the voices from the street. Michael gives us this voice and with passion, humour, intellectual curiosity, and insight—all supported with creditable research.

Did you know that you can go to jail for throwing a snowball in Manitoba? Did you know that "if someone is dying in front of you, you're not legally bound to help (except in Quebec), but you must call the police if they talk about breaking the law" (20)? Michael reveals many such interesting observations as these while he offers a wealth of good practical advice for anyone involved in the 'McJustice system.' For instance, Michael explains why, upon arrest, you need to first obtain bail and then have your lawyer negotiate an easing of the conditions a month or two later. Or, he offers the fact that should your lawyer arrange a plea bargain in which the prosecution agrees to drop all charges except one, this does not mean the dropped charges disappear. Indeed, they may reappear: for instance, when you are applying for parole and the parole board sees the 'dropped charges' in your file.

Michael frequently intersperses his observations and considered comments with quotes from philosophers and learned intellectuals to succinctly illustrate his points. For instance, quoting William Pitt, "Necessity is the plea for every infringement of freedom. It is the argument of tyrants; it is the creed of slaves" (16). He says that he doesn't watch TV but spends his time reading and learning. It is evident that Michael knows his stuff and at times he surprised me with his observations, even though I have been teaching criminal justice system courses for close to 20 years and I am a former prisoner myself.

Michael takes an unequivocal position on the failures of Canada's system of injustice. He makes clear how the fear of crime is furthered through the media and entertainment industry and how "More laws, prisoners, and tax dollars mean more security and financial gain" for them (148). Further, he writes,

> I find it very odd how the wrongfully accused or convicted who eventually win an appeal can say the system works. If the system really works, they should not have been charged or convicted in the first place. (141)

However, he also offers informed instruction on how we could better achieve public safety and community integration. Michael borrows from Michel Foucault to show that "the ceremony of punishment ... is an exercise of 'terror' to make everyone aware, through the body of the offender, of the might and power of the law and justice system" (133). Michael explains how Canada's current 'tough on crime' legislation makes "it easier for the 'professionals' of the justice system to steal away the conflict, thereby robbing local communities of their ability to face trouble and restore peace" (108). He contrasts this retributive approach to "community projects of restorative justice [that allow] healing, reconciliation, and giving back to the community" (109). He cites Professor Alan Young, "Compassion requires emotional engagement inconsistent with the adversarial ethic" (111). Michael argues for community-based approaches to public safety showing how programs delivered in the community are far more effective than those offered in a prison. Yet, parole and other forms of conditional release have been plummeting in recent decades.

As Michael states, only Russia and the United States surpass Canada's incarceration rate. He notes how correctional programs in prison can actually "increase the likelihood of offending" (207). Not what most Canadian citizens would expect from their tax dollars. Michael illustrates doing time in segregation or the punishment cells.

> One popular conception of time in the hole is that it drags by ever so slowly but seems to have flashed by in the end. It's a weird thing to explain. It seems to drag because you sit and stare at a blank wall all day or pace for hours. It's what I did for twenty-eight straight months. It was the insanity of such boredom that led me to begin

writing these words. When the end comes, it's as if it passed in a blink (196).

This book by C.W. Michael is written from a place of informed thought and hard experience and deserves wide exposure. It is not only 'a practical guide to surviving arrest in Canada' but is an excellent text for courses in criminal justice as well as a resource for anyone wanting a meaningful understanding of Canada's system of arrest, trial and punishment.

This book is accessible and fun to read. It is entertaining and illuminating and it is a read that goes by 'in a blink.' I was left wondering why such a fine writer would want to remain anonymous and use a pseudonym. I felt excited, illuminated, and aroused by the images and I couldn't put the book down. Recommended.

REFERENCES

Michael, C.W. (2012). *The Criminal's Handbook: A Practical Guide to Surviving Arrest in Canada.* London, ONT: Insomniac Press.

□ ◊ □□ ◊ □□ ◊ □

The Anti-Capitalist Resistance Comic Book
Hill, Gord.
Foreword by Allan Antliff;
Introduction by Dave Cunningham
(Vancouver: Arsenal Pulp Press, 2012. 96 pages.)

Reviewed by—Mike Larsen,
Kwantlen Polytechnic University, June 2013.

Gord Hill's *The Anti-Capitalist Resistance Comic Book* presents a narrative account of the history of anti-capitalist mobilization from the standpoint of participants involved in direct action. Hill stops short of explicitly identifying himself as one of the central characters, but there is an autobiographical tone to the

work: most of the events depicted in *The Anti-Capitalist
Resistance Comic Book* are
seen from the perspective of
militant members of Indigenous, anarchist, and anti-capitalist social movements who
hail from occupied Coast Salish
territory.

The book (written and il-
lustrated by Hill) is composed
of a collection of comics of
varying lengths, each documenting a particular conver-
gence or action. It is organized in chronological order,
with a focus on events following the rise of the anti-globalization movement during the 1990s. With a few exceptions (notably the J18 '99 Carnival Against Capital and the Battle in
Seattle), the events chronicled in *The Anti-Capitalist Resistance
Comic Book* take place in Canada. The 2001 Quebec City Summit of the Americas, 2010 Vancouver Anti-Olympic Campaign,
and 2010 Toronto G20 Summit are profiled at length. Readers
get a glimpse at some of the conversations between activists
that take place in the lead-up to actions (especially prior to the
2010 Olympics), but the majority of the book focuses on moments of public confrontation between members of social
movements and authorities—occupations, marches, and running street battles.

The Anti-Capitalist Resistance Comic Book opens with a
short, helpful prologue on the historical linkages between capitalism and colonialism. The prologue invites readers to situate
the book's account of late modern anti-capitalist struggles in a
broader socio-historical context, and it introduces one of Hill's
main themes, as noted in the foreword by author Allan Antliff:

> Addressing what he is fighting for, Gord begins his narrative with
> tribal ways of life prior to the imposition of state power, and rightly
> so. Indigenous affinities with anarchism reside not only in a shared
> recognition that state power and exploitation are flip sides of the
> same coin: decentralizing power so as to renew societal ways of life

attuned to nature in all its diversity is the heart of the matter for Indigenous peoples and anarchists alike. (9)

Hill regards Indigenous anti-colonial struggles and anti-capitalist resistance as being naturally and inextricably entwined, and
historically rooted in the central role that the European colonization of the Americas played in the expansion of capital and
empire. This is a theme that is explored at length in Hill's previous work, *The 500 Years of Resistance Comic Book* (2010).
The two books are complimentary, and combined they offer a
provocative challenge to the dominant historical narratives of
settlement and globalization.

Another key theme addressed in *The Anti-Capitalist Resistance Comic Book* is the heterogeneous nature of the anti-globalization movement, exemplified in the fault lines that exist between actors and groups with different perspectives on the mer-
its of diversity of tactics, street theatre, collaboration with authorities in the organization of events, and the broader reform
vs. revolution debate. Hill is an outspoken proponent of both
peaceful protest and militant action, but an opponent of dog-
matic pacifism and reformism. In *The Anti-Capitalist Resistance Comic Book*, his criticism of liberal left perspectives often takes the form of satire. In one scene, during the Battle in
Seattle, militants participating in a Black Bloc are confronted
by a self-proclaimed 'legitimate protester' who opposes their
engagement in property destruction. Having failed to convince
the militants to desist in window-smashing, the protester attempts to physically restrain them, prompting an observer to re-
mark "Pacifists. Some of 'em are violently opposed to property
destruction. No respect for diversity" (34). Towards the end of
the book Hill criticizes the bureaucratic nature of the Occupy
organizing model through a depiction of an occupier addressing
a group and saying "I propose we make a new committee to
discuss the issue and, failing to then reach a decision, make a
sub-committee to further debate the issue and then bring it to
the general assembly ..." (94). Both of these scenes provide
fruitful launching points for discussion and debate.

Hill's black-and-white graphic art is characterful and unclut-
tered. The illustrated panels mesh well with the textual narrative, emphasizing action, conflict, and the physicality of the
struggles depicted. Throughout the book, Hill incorporates pan-

els that reproduce iconic photographs of events, including the image of Tommie Smith and John Carlos giving the Black Power salute during their medal ceremony at the 1968 Olympic Games, the assault on the mesh fence and enthusiastic use of pepper spray by police at the 1997 APEC summit, and the image of a masked and helmeted cop stomping on the back of a seated protester during the 2010 G20.

These panels serve as welcome intersections between *The Anti-Capitalist Resistance Comic Book* and other representations of events. I recently used an excerpt from Hill's account of the events surrounding the Toronto 2010 G20 as a reading in a class on violence in the context of 'summit policing', and invited my students to seek out some of the photographs and videos that are reflected in the comic. Each time a panel was 'matched' to another image in this way a fruitful discussion ensued. We explored the context surrounding the image, discussed the authenticity of the representation, and talked about other images that could serve as inspiration for new panels.

By way of constructive criticism (and perhaps a suggestion for future projects), there is room in *The Anti-Capitalist Resistance Comic Book* for additional coverage of some key issues. The impact of the state reaction to the events of 11 September 2001 on both policing and anti-capitalist organizing, for instance, deserves more than the single page it gets, for example. Some additional discussion of the implications of the surveillance and infiltration of social movements by police and security agencies would also be beneficial. For the most part, 'the authorities' depicted in *The Anti-Capitalist Resistance Comic Book* are clearly recognizable as such, as most are wearing militaristic uniforms and riot gear. Hill's style is highly effective at emphasizing the distinctions between visibly-identifiable factions (black-clad cops, participants in Black Bloc actions, and non-militant protesters are easy to pick out), and it would be interesting to see him address the more ambiguous shapes that the politics of class conflict can and does take.

If Hill's objective with *The Anti-Capitalist Resistance Comic Book* is to provide a provocative, radical, view-from-the-streets introduction to the recent history and broader context associated with anti-capitalist resistance, he has definitely succeeded. This is not—and is not intended to be—a comprehensive overview or in-depth analysis. As Hill (2010: 6) has previously noted, "[t]he strength of the comic book is that it uses minimal text with graphic art to tell the story. This format is useful in reaching children, youth, and adults who have a hard time reading books or lengthy articles". Beyond these audiences, *The Anti-Capitalist Resistance Comic Book* will be of interest to activists and educators interested in supplementing and expanding traditional literacies through the incorporation of graphic narrative.

References

Hill, Gord (2010). *The 500 Years of Resistance Comic Book*. Vancouver: Arsenal Pulp Press.

Hill, Gord (2012). *The Anti-Capitalist Resistance Comic Book*. Vancouver: Arsenal Pulp Press.

□ ◊ □□ ◊ □□ ◊ □

State Power and Democracy: Before and During the Presidency of George W. Bush
Kolin, Andrew.
(New York: Palgrave Macmillan, 2011. 262 pages.)

Reviewed by—G.G. Preparata,
Pontifical Gregorian University, April 2013

In roughly 200 pages, A. Kolin's State Power and Democracy is designed to offer a supple chronological account of the process that has—gradually but steadily—transformed America's early colonial commonwealth into a full-blown technocratic and authoritarian (and, one might add, nightmarish) system.

The book's simple thesis is reiterated, chapter after chapter, by showing

STATE POWER
AND
DEMOCRACY
BEFORE AND DURING THE PRESIDENCY
OF GEORGE W. BUSH

ANDREW KOLIN

how, from the outset, America was conceived as an elitist structure whose constitutional concern was, de facto, to render the
crucial governing mechanisms of the newly-founded, and vi-
brant, "democracy" (in name only), as stringently undemocratic
as possible. In other words, the thesis seems to imply that the
United States has always been a (nasty) monarchy in disguise,
and that the deceit has become irremediably patent with the ad-
vent and post-9/11 politics and policies of George W. Bush
(2000-2008): under this king, Bush II, it so seems that the child
could thus be heard crying 'the democracy has no clothes, long
live the President'.

The initial chapter details how, in the minds of the (aristo-
cratic) framers of the republic, political representation was di-
luted and made as indirect and roundabout as institutionally
feasible so as to shield the sacredness of property from whatever sort of populist land-grabbing menace, all the while no
(genocidal and larcenous) effort was spared to despoil entirely
the Natives of any possession the Anglo-Saxon Whites could
have naturally exploited to their advantage and behoof.

The argumentation is subsequently compounded by an item-
ized discussion of the slew of patriotic acts that have accompanied America ever since her eventual, and fateful, imperial initi-
ation in the late nineteenth century with the manufactured
provocations against Spain in Cuba and the Philippines. There
and then also began the Yankee tradition of torture and gratu-
itous deeds of ferocity perpetrated by American troops against
indigenous populations—the precursors, so to speak, to the notorious and widely-publicized slaughters of Vietnam and the
more recent, pornographic abuses of Abu Ghraib and Gitmo.
All of which goes into making the book's narrative a synopsis
of America's: 1) elite-inspired anti-democratic bills—cravenly
approved by an ever-more delegitimized House of cowering
Representatives; 2) viciously centralizing executive; 3) sadistic
use of violence upon weaker, colonized "others"; 4) avowed
and aggressive imperialism in concomitance with foul-play in
the arena of international law; and 5) tightening surveillance
chokehold on the nation's privacy.

In this connection, Hoover's FBI receives brief but diligent
mention, as do, e.g., the NSA, the CIA, the School of the Americas (now more verbosely named Western Hemisphere Institute

for Security Cooperation), and all those other sinister US government agencies that have come to be ominously featured in works of alarmed dissent such as this one.

The virtual effacement of the democratic process is recounted through the defining phases of the nation's recent history, from the olden days of anarchism (1880s-1920s) to the late War on Terror (2001 to the present) against Islamism and all other "rogue" formations, by way of the various authoritarian, "fascistic" "national security" acts passed during the tantalizing occasions of the Cold War (viz. the Red Scare; McCarthyism and the House of Un-American Activities Committee; the shadow of the "military-industrial complex"; or the tough confrontation between Nixon's executive and revolutionaries of the Counter-culture). The ambivalent, post-Soviet beginning of terrorism's second wave, itself split as it was between the putative skullduggery of Islamism (the 1993 attack at the World Trade Center) and the no less enigmatic, yet short-lived, skirmish opposing federal agencies (the ATF etc.) to America's very own Right-wing militias (which culminated in the Oklahoma City bombing of 1995), is another important segment of this story, which the book does not omit.

Particular attention is devoted to the tenure of Bush Jr., which the author, quite evidently, considers exceptional in point of boldness, far-reaching transformation, unscrupulousness, and, in an important sense, in point of candor—as the nation's last-standing vestiges of "freedom": freedom from arbitrary intrusion, seizure, silencing, and incarceration—were, according to the author, shamelessly crushed by the executive of Bush II in a state of anti-terrorist exception.

Noticing, moreover, that under President Barack Obama, despite his grandiloquent oath to reform the government, no reversal of what appears to be a most potent and unambiguous push for the creation of an all-perfect "police State" has taken place, the author cannot but entertain pessimistic conclusions. According to Kolin, the only hope to see this catastrophic process hindered and eventually defeated would hinge on the ability of the American people to re-appropriate somehow the institution of due process and re-establish this key, democratic practice, by bringing to justice, first of all, the very members of Bush II's, de facto criminal, executive.

Pious wish.

In sum, Kolin's State Power and Democracy is a standard (leftist) recital of America's anti-democratic pedigree. To remind—even in the stenographic and somewhat too notional manner of this primer—newer generations of students of the ways in which brutality and the cult of violence insinuate themselves in the institutional vicissitudes of a country is good and proper. Compassion is to be nurtured also by exposing how the logic of prevarication, of injustice and racism, crystallizes over time, and the peculiar social and cultural conditions under which it does so. There are already a great many books like this one on the shelves (say, à la Chomsky or Zinn): one more does not add significantly to our feeling and understanding of the spiritual perils which the dominance of the USA, in its present countenance, poses for the world at large, but it certainly does no harm—quite the opposite, in fact.

The problem lies elsewhere. On a more general level, the structure of the book, terse as it is, affords no opportunity to seize on any kind of "law" governing this disquieting transformation. In other words, all the information presented in this particular sequence and format does not enable one to understand anything more about the evolution of politics and society in America as a result of this pressure on the part of the elite to shield its privilege.

One could ask, for instance: who/what was Edgar Hoover, truly? And why did he come in power when he did, and in the way he did (i.e., hounding European anarchist expatriates)? Alternatively, there is no sense whatever of how the relentless reinforcement of America's police's apparatus affected, or was affected in turn, by the crime dynamics of the country in the last 110 years or so. And how does the industrial-military complex fit in in all this? Is this a question of empire or proletarian control? Consider the episode of the Cold War: was it devised to strengthen the elite, or did the latter just exploit it to its own proprietary ends? Was there actual "communism" in the USA? Or was it a mere façade which inquisitors used to pursue political enemies? And if so, who were these "enemies"? Dissenters? What kinds? Foreign or domestic, rich or poor? Where there (elite) factions at play? Why, say, was McCarthy's witch-hunt stopped quite suddenly after a spectacular launch? Or, to return to Bush Jr.: if, indeed, conspicuous seeds of a fully militarized police-regime had been planted by his Democrat predecessor, Bill Clinton, what could account, under Bush, for such a stark contrast in the "air" one breathed in America after 9/11? What of Zeitgeist?

These are not idle questions, because knowing events in succession helps only insofar as these events punctuate a particular plot, a particular story. So, beyond the stereotypical account of a leadership jealous of its prerogatives, what is the actual story behind America's hardening of authoritarian resolve? The book does not say. For, in the end, being told that a regime, which is assumed to be intrinsically monarchic, has been issuing tyrannical, undemocratic edicts for more than a century is hardly a revelation. What is interesting, instead, is to discern and explain the trajectory of a particular nation in time, as a socio-cultural whole: the problem is not that of relaying history in the form of a chronicle with which to mark the putative stages of a viciously anti-democratic process, but rather that of understanding how a society possessed of such a cult of privilege and violence, like America's, comes to shape its own history.

And this—i.e. the "true visage" of history—is the crucial aspect of the problem, because a US patriot could very well retort that, deeply unfortunate or sinister as all these developments might have been for the civil liberties and rights of the average American citizen, they were all painfully necessary in order to protect and safeguard the collectivity. And couched in these terms, the patriotic apologia is unbreachable. If anarchists, militias, terrorists, Soviets, and Islamists are believed to be (more or less) dangerously "real," as much as the patriot believes them to be, then, there is only room, if any, to quibble on the actual range to which the government may legitimately extend the radius of intrusion upon the life of its residents. And, in this case, the residual impression of a book's like Kolin's is that, in all times and circumstances, the US government has brooked on this issue (namely, the discretionary extent of its purview to guarantee "national security") no debate whatsoever. Unfortunate indeed, but the overarching intimation seems to be that it has been for the best of us all: State authority, so runs the patriotic adage, might have occasionally acted roughly and questionably, but in the vast majority of cases it did so in our collective interest. Posited thus, the issue can only be, at best, moot, and, as a result, the labor of denunciation of the unskeptical leftist, at worst, nugatory.

It is only when dissenting scholars will have conclusively and extensively shown that, to this day, these predatory and criminal elites have been fabricating, as a matter of routine, these foes and these crises with a view to implement their liberticidal ploys; it is only then that academic denunciations such as Kolin's will acquire proper relief (Kolin acknowledges the mendacious, conspiratorial trigger of the Spanish-American and Vietnam wars, as well as the grand little show prior to the second Iraq invasion of 2003—yet these are hardly controversial; they're in the historiographical mainstream—and appears to take everything else at face value). Because without such a convincing and widely-disseminated proof, the defenders of the regime will always be able to justify any crime or reprisal— even the most indescribable, such as, e.g., the 500,000 Iraqi children killed by the regime of UN sanctions in the early 1990s—by agitating the token specter (in the above instance, the need to oppose the "evil" of Saddam Hussein and suffer these deaths as a tough "price to pay"—we all remember Madeleine Albright's unforgettable declaration) and mute the credulous critics thereby.

So, in the end, the bulk of the work still remains to be done, and the hardest questions to be answered. Again: what was the Cold War? Was it really this alleged East-West contraposition? Who/what role was Edgar Hoover supposed to play and to what end? And McCarthy? Was there ever a threat from Afghanistan? Have we been told the truth about 9/11? Etc.

And once we will have found the answers to these questions, we will be able to interpret with precision the actual drift, timing and duration of the various institutional steps and phases sedulously undertaken by the elites to obliterate systematically any left-over margin from which one may attempt to manifest (non-violent) opposition to their barbarous rule.

Guido G. Preparata
Rome, Italy, 23 April

□ ◊ □□ ◊ □□ ◊ □

Defying the Tomb.
Johnson, Kevin "Rashid."
Forward by Russell "Maroon" Shoats
Afterword by Sundiata Acoli
Introduction & Afterword by Tom Big Warrior
(Montréal: Kersplebedeb, 2010. 387 pages.)

Reviewed by—Jeff Shantz,
Kwantlen Polytechnic University, July 2013

There has grown over the last several decades a real disjuncture between working class communities and movements and political prisoners. Even activists have largely lost touch with those comrades imprisoned for organizing only a generation or two before.

That situation is recently changing, perhaps in fundamental ways. As the state clampdown on alternative globalization activists and organizers grows, and as community organizers face jail time under extreme charges such as conspiracy, it is inevitable that more people from contemporary movements will find themselves inside prisons as political prisoners—or will be required to support comrades who have been taken inside.

During the period from the 1980s up to the first decades of the twenty-first century, the lessons, experiences, words, and guidance of political prisoners were kept alive by the efforts of a few dedicated people and groups, such as the Anarchist Black Cross, the anarchist producers of the "Certain Days" political prisoners support calendar, and the publisher of armed struggle literature Kersplebedeb.

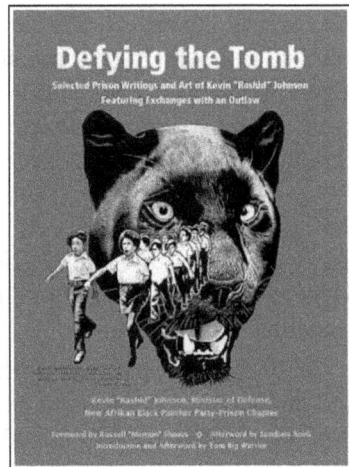

At this point in time, with increasingly repressive criminal justice policies and practices there are clearly obstacles to collaboration between prisoners and outsiders in the growing resistance to global capital. Yet, this repression will bring new activists into the prisons and open opportunities for overcoming some of the physical barriers to interaction. More and more the politically mobilized will be compelled to engage with and learn from those members of our movements who have been imprisoned. Thankfully there are works like *Defying the Tomb* that insurgents can turn to for analysis and information.

The author, and the others involved in the collection (Russell "Maroon" Shoats, Sundiata Acoli, and Tom Big Warrior) bring several decades of experience each to bear on the issues. These include experiences of armed struggle and militant resistance. It is important to be reminded of a period, not that long ago, when police were subjected to retaliation for their murders of African American youth and activists.

Throughout the work offers a much needed class analysis of current social problems. It is refreshing to see capitalism identified directly and clearly as the issue throughout, rather than neoliberalism, crisis, or austerity, which are symptoms of capitalist development and regulation. The struggle for political prisoners, and against prisons, is also an anti-capitalist struggle. As Johnson and the others in this work insist, it is necessary that we recognize the unity of the struggle against racist oppression and the class struggle for socialist revolution (and the place of criminal justice systems within these struggles).

Defying the Tomb provides a useful discussion of histories of Pan-Africanist struggle and its intersections with anti-capitalism, and communism more proactively. Indeed, the "Foreword" by Russell "Maroon" Shoats offers an excellent introduction and overview to the history of Pan-Africanist and revolutionary black liberation movements. It alone is worth the read for anyone looking for an interesting primer to recent black liberation politics and their intersections with communism.

The first section offers biographical sketches of Rashid and another young prisoner Outlaw. This sets the stage for the conversation in letters between the two men that makes up the middle, largest, section of the collection. Rashid was imprisoned for 16 years at the time of writing (2006) going in at the age of 18. He had spent the spent the previous 12 years in solitary. His imprisonment resulted from his targeting as a cop killer. The biographical section details his growth and transformation from lumpen youth involved in street crimes (mostly drug trade) to proletarian revolutionary organizer. These are familiar transformations for those of us who grow up poor and working class. They are stories of the shift from individual anger, resentment, and rebellion to collective action and revolutionary struggle. It is the process of finding voice—of finding the words to articulate, analyze, and understand what had previously been inchoate feelings of frustration, a sense that something is wrong but needing to name it.

In his writings on prison Johnson outlines in detail the systematic abuses heaped on prisoners and the attempts by guards to divide prisoners against each other through violence. He also shows the successes of organizing solidarity among prisoners and united defense against guards. Collective organizing against guards is effective in halting abuses—indeed it is the only reliable approach.

Along the way he came to learn that using the courts would not produce continuous results in changing abusive conditions. He taught himself law and became effective in litigation, though never gaining the results desired in reducing or removing abuses. Direct action was needed primarily, but its effects were limited where it involves single rebellious prisoners. He came to recognize that the conditions in prison—indeed the very existence of prisons—could not be changed without fundamental changes in socioeconomic conditions—the broader social structures of capitalism. He went from reformer to abolitionist—a move from a critical to a radical criminological perspective.

His study of revolutionary theory began in 2001 (11 years in) and was highly influenced, as has been the case for many prisoners, by the works of George Jackson. George Jackson plays an important part in the political education and coming to class consciousness of both Rashid and Outlaw.

Outlaw offers poignant counters to the morality that regulates the working class poor and which is echoed in most of mainstream criminology. He suggests:

These were the contradictions in my life, the contradiction between poverty and morality. Morality would have you obey the law, respect authority and so forth. But you may not be able to escape poverty without breaking the law, at least to some degree. We are told to seek legal means to meet our needs, but how are these needs to be met? The ruling powers tell us poor lower-class folks that we have an obligation, a social responsibility to society, to abide by the law, but they don't have any social responsibility to us to help us meet our needs. It's pure bourgeoisie class-based morality, a morality that serves the ruling class, not the masses of the oppressed. (59–60)

Rashid asserts the necessity of organized mass struggle in overcoming oppression and offers lessons from his close reading of theory and history and his own organizing efforts under highly restricted conditions. In his view characteristics of extremism and a willingness to suffer must go hand in hand with uncompromising tactical approaches. He believes these characteristics to be largely absent from the Left in the US.

Personal commitment is not enough. There is a need for shared ideas—for ideology. In the absence of such it is easy for people to lose the initiative to struggle. If action is based in a strong character or instigator, the momentum dissipates when that character is removed or transferred.

On individualism and class Outlaw suggests:

Under the influence of illegitimate-capitalist values, I was pursuing the alleviation of social-economic hardship through individual advancement. This is a wholly inadequate remedy to social problems because it doesn't challenge the fundamental injustice of class-exploitation and class-oppression, which are responsible for creating the socio-economic ills in the first place. Unaware of my class interest, I was perpetuating my own oppression by engaging in competitive capitalist practices that ensure the smooth functioning of the system as the exploiting minority profits in more ways than one off the division and disunity engendered by competition, so prevalent among the exploited. Look around: competition, euphemistically called "individuality," permeates and is systematically promoted to the masses of people while the corporate conglomerates and Fortune 500 are busy "merging and monopolizing. (75)

The contributors are firm in insisting that those who struggle against states and capital must be prepared to defend themselves. To understand the nature of the state is to know that it will attack to kill when and where it feels a threat to its authority and power. In their view, one that is often eschewed these days, revolutionary mass struggle must be military as well as economic, political, and cultural. It must be mass based. The absence of any of these factors leads to failure as the study of past revolutions suggests. Resisting cultural domination, a favored preoccupation of much of the late twentieth and early twenty-first century Left and alternative globalization movements, is no substitute for resisting economic, political, and military domination.

Even under the most brutal military powers of imperialism, resistance forces can succeed by building a secure base among the people (30). This is achieved through the establishment of economic programs that serve the needs of the population. These programs are what I call infrastructures of resistance. They include schools, health clinics, food distribution centers, and so on. The US and Canada are massive spaces, with areas less accessible to security forces yet with access to vast resources. The working class and oppressed must develop united structures to coordinate their work and to bring together often isolated organizers. Mass based infrastructures are needed within the oppressed sections of the working class.

Rashid rightly points out that most people from "our social sector," the working class, cannot even shoot a handgun, let alone use real weaponry in any combat capacity that would inevitably be required in a real uprising.

Outlaw notes that while the radical Left cannot shoot straight, Right wing militias and National Rifle Association members "are dangerously proficient" (87).

At the same time Rashid argues that the class character of Right wing militias and survivalists suggests that some might be potential allies. They have an inchoate and confused opposition to monopoly capitalism. It is obscured by conspiracy theories, paranoia, and religious fundamentalism and clearly needs some ideological education.

There must be tangible victories and material gains. People must see results and have reason to believe that organizing and active participation within social struggles *will* improve their lives in real and meaningful ways. The organizers must be able to help people and their communities to develop capacities to provide for material needs "which the enemy state cannot and will not provide" (91). The community survival programs organized by the Black Panther Party in cities throughout the US provide important examples of this.

Revolutionaries must be connected to communities of the working class and poor. People respond positively to revolutionary ideals when they can see the realistic possibility of success. Where they fight and win their confidence and morale increase. Where they lose repeatedly their commitment wanes. Repeated losses condition people to believe they cannot win. It leads to defeatism and avoidance.

When organizers are not prepared to fight, they are easily put down by authorities. This, then, reinforces the belief that movements cannot win. Organizing without preparing for revolutionary self-defense against authorities is actually preparing people to be defeatist. Failure reinforces conditioned pessimism. As Johnson suggests:

And when we did dare to defy the odds (with total lack of coordinated unity and attention to strategy, tactics, and logistics), we were conditioned to believe (with some justification) that their reflex violence, their revenge, would be so brutal and widespread that the resulting suffering which our resistance provoked wasn't worth the effort. Therefore—failure leading to pessimism—any idea of waging a successful struggle for mass freedom was neutralized." (142–143)

There must be clear functionalist solutions developed. Movements require "social service programs through which to materially reach the broad masses, showing them the need for struggle and giving them something to fight for" (133). Anticapitalist organizers must get their hands dirty in mass-based projects. They must organize people around meeting their own needs. It is not enough to engage in agitational work, as in periods of low struggle or demobilization perhaps. A critical analysis of capitalism and imperialism is not sufficient.

Perhaps the most debated aspects of the book will be the emphasis on armed struggle. For Johnson, the failure of previous mobilizations in the US has been partly a failure to mobilize "an armed mass base" (133). He argues that politics takes primacy in armed struggle. The main purpose of armed struggle is to protect political work and workers, not only to destroy the enemy's forces (134). Armed struggle or insurrection in an advanced capitalist context cannot operate without a mass base. Securing that base requires established and durable infrastructures of resistance. Guerrilla actions without a mass based political movement are futile.

Broad mass appeal and support come through meeting needs and securing victories. Health clinics, schools, clothing and food provision, and community facilities and youth recreation are some of the services provided. Many who join movements do so out of the desire to find community or security rather than adherence to the specific principles espoused by the movements. Organized alternatives must, in part, be able to offer a sense of belonging and community. For Johnson: "People can be mobilized to support or at least be neutral toward, most any cause—even something as counterproductive as an open-air neighborhood drug market—if they're given a sense of objective benefit, security, and community" (161).

Once people see that establishment structures are unwilling or unable to meet basic needs—and alternatives become available—they will struggle to break from those structures.

Authorities are aware of this and typically respond with repression in cases where this appears to be happening, even in the early stages. The example of the state response to Occupy movements in various cities is but one recent case in point.

There is a pressing need to develop and organize base of logistical support that can mobilize, support, and sustain what might become revolutionary struggle rather than seeing discontent dissipate in ineffectual, but cathartic, insurrections or riots. Uprisings and rebellions can be extended and given lengthier duration and more positively impactful outcomes. Small groups cannot, despite the best wishes of insurrectionist, provoke mass uprisings or "manufacture revolution," or construct the conditions that will lead to mass rebellion.

Those who suggest they oppose or fear working class involvement in armed struggle forget or avoid the fact that the working class provides most of the combatants in armed struggle (war) in the US and Canada—unfortunately fighting *for* their oppressors. The revolutionary armed struggle simply sees them fighting *against* their oppressors to gain their own independence and self-determination.

Prisons have been an essential tool in state capitalist capacity to manufacture discontinuity in popular struggles. Imprisonment has broken the link between struggles of the 1960s and 1970s and today. At the same time this discontinuity has allowed for the expansion and consolidation of state capitalist rule (290). This weapon has been deployed especially against Blacks and Natives in the US and Canada respectively. It has made prisoners of political activists and organizers.

There will be dedicated efforts by states and capital to isolate the armed front from the masses.

In the 1960s and 1970s, Daniel Patrick Moynihan advised the Nixon administration to achieve this goal partly by criminalizing the image of the armed front. As today, revolutionary activity became constructed as terrorism. Concerted efforts were also put into dissolving the lower strata grassroots support and replacing it with middle class social conformity and moralism.

The "war on crime" initiated first under Nixon, was directed at stopping the spread of organized armed resistance and the militant tactics of working class and poor youth, particularly Black youth. Under NSC 46 the government explicitly stated that continued growth of Black struggles for economic justice in the 1970s would require violent repression from the government to stabilize the social relations of working class and poor communities. NSC 46 noted that such steps would be "misunderstood" both inside and outside the US and could lead to further trouble for the administration (314).

Middle strata elites, with interests in access to and maintenance of capitalist markets, undermine and eventually replace working class and poor people among the grassroots leadership. Revolutionary activities and armed struggle tactics are demonized and degraded. Existing institutions are presented as means for meeting social needs and energies are channeled toward statist or market based institutions and practices.

Infrastructures of resistance provide a logistical base for building mass support. Many of these infrastructures were destroyed and/or demobilized following the state repression against the upsurge of the late 1960s and early 1970s. The "war on crime" played a part in this. As Johnson notes:

> The ensuing mass incarceration, criminalization, concentration of police and surveillance, and the vast Prison-Industrial Complex targeted especially at poor, urban Blacks, has been a conscious tactical response of empire to repress anti-colonial, anti-capitalist, and revolutionary fervor amongst the oppressed classes. (298–299)

Ironically, perhaps, it was only in prison that they gained access to the literature that would help them properly understand their experiences. This revolutionary theory was itself brought into prison environments as a result of the mass incarcerations of political prisoners in the 1960s and 1970s, including members of the Black Panther Party, American Indian Movement, and Black Liberation Army.

It is a reflection on social conditions that prisons have been sites of revolutionary upsurge in the neoliberal period. Prison populations have expanded exponentially over the last 30 years as incarceration has replaced social housing and other programs that addressed, if inadequately, pressing social issues like poverty. This is a class war and there are many POWs.

On the whole, this is an exciting and enlightening collection of essays and letters. It reveals a uniquely energetic analysis of contemporary issues that are of pressing concern for anyone pursuing social justice and a better world. Some of the issues discussed include revolutionary strategy and tactics, class inequality, racism, prison practices, impediments to solidarity among the oppressed, movement histories, and psychology. The book also provides invaluable insights into the experiences of politically active prisoners *within* the prison system in the US.

Both the cover and the dedication page include a single quote from Franz Fanon: "Each generation must, out of relative obscurity, discover its mission, and fulfill it or betray it." The current generation is still struggling toward this task. The current collection will certainly help in this process and offers useful guidance along the way forward.

Radical Criminology, a new journal of theory and practice for struggle

Considering contributing to an upcoming issue?

Authors are encouraged to submit articles for publication, directly to our website:
http://journal.radicalcriminology.org

We are actively seeking marginalized voices, not only in the field of critical criminological scholarship, but also artists, activists, and reviewers. Or, send us a letter!

All academic articles are subject to a blind peer review process. (This does not include "insurgencies," artwork, poetry and book reviews, which will be assessed by our editorial committee.)

Please visit our website for more detailed submission guidelines. (There are no submission nor publication fees.) Create a reader and author account there now...

We use the Public Knowledge Project's 'open journal' online submission system (http://pkp.sfu.ca/ojs), which allows authors to submit papers via the Web. This system speeds up the submission and review process, and allows you to view the status of your paper online.

Artwork, poetic submissions, and notes on insurgencies can also be posted to our website, e-mailed to <editors@radicalcriminology.org> or send us mail at:
Radical Criminology,
ATTN: Jeff Shantz, Dept. of Criminology,
Kwantlen Polytechnic University
12666 72nd Ave,
Surrey, B.C. V3W 2M8

(and on twitter..find us @critcrim)

www.ingramcontent.com/pod-product-compliance
Lightning Source LLC
Chambersburg PA
CBHW050653270326
41927CB00012B/3003